VIV GRAHAM

DORS

.col.

.com

POT OldTymeBullDog.com

DB ° 07976977521

ending £400

Fred

graig park

Steve/Barnet

Bosanmonth

Duckning

DS/

MILFORDS

1   2 TON gritsand

VIV
GRAHAM

STEPHEN RICHARDS

JOHN BLAKE

Published by John Blake Publishing Ltd,
3, Bramber Court, 2 Bramber Road,
London W14 9PB, England

www.blake.co.uk

First published in hardback in 2005

ISBN 1 84454 127 4

British Library Cataloguing-in-Publication Data:

A catalogue record for this book is available from the British Library.

Design by www.envydesign.co.uk

Printed in Great Britain by Bookmarque

1 3 5 7 9 10 8 6 4 2

Papers used by John Blake Publishing are natural, recyclable products made
from wood grown in sustainable forests. The manufacturing processes
conform to the environmental regulations of the country of origin.

Every attempt has been made to contact the relevant copyright-holders, but
some were unobtainable. We would be grateful if the appropriate people
could contact us.

For Asil Nadir. Hopefully the truth will eventually come
out and you can return to the UK and win.

OTHER TITLES BY STEPHEN RICHARDS

Insanity: My Mad Life
by Charles Bronson with Stephen Richards

The Krays and Me
by Charles Bronson with Stephen Richards

The Good Prison Guide
by Charles Bronson with Stephen Richards

The Lost Girl
by Caroline Roberts with Stephen Richards

It's Criminal
by Stephen Richards

Born to Fight
by Richy Horsley with Stephen Richards

Street Warrior
by Malcolm Price with Stephen Richards

Crash 'n' Carry
by Stephen Richards

The Taxman
by Brian Cockerill with Stephen Richards

Lost in Care
by Jimmy Holland with Stephen Richards

CONTENTS

FOREWORD

Viv has always been a friend of mine. When visiting Newcastle I would sometimes come across Viv when he was in Macey's nightclub and I would stand with him and have a few drinks (as a friend, not as my minder).

Viv asked me if I could get him a signed football as I was playing for Newcastle at that time. I was happy to oblige.

I was devastated by news of him being killed (as I would be about this happening to anyone I knew).

Gazza (Newcastle United, Tottenham, Lazio, Glasgow Rangers, Middlesbrough and England)

INTRODUCTION:
THE LAST WARRIOR

People talked in hushed voices about the shooting of Viv Graham. He was someone nearly everyone knew. A legend in his lifetime, he worked his way to the very top of the criminal elite in the North-East of England, until his iron grip on its activities extended to the darkest corner of the underworld.

With a name like Viv, he might have expected some ribbing, but the brutality surrounding this hard man soon dispelled any thought people had of feminine charm.

Viv Graham was murdered on New Year's Eve 1993, shot down in cold blood, assassinated by his own underworld associates who had become his enemy during his reign. He died from two gunshot wounds that tore his insides to bits. He lived violently and he died violently.

Long before the police revealed the victim's name, his identity was known to local residents. The underworld talked freely among themselves but fell silent when approached by reporters. Even taxi drivers were quick to tell their fares, 'Viv Graham's been shot.'

That night and into the early hours of the following morning, there was a sense of unease; roads were strangely quiet because of the police cordon erected where Viv had been shot.

A man with a solid but unspoken code of conduct, Viv was an underworld enforcer: big, strong and capable of giving more than he received when it came to hands-on action. He prided himself on his ability to fight with bare fists instead of weapons. Fear and respect were part and parcel of Viv's everyday life. If you didn't inspire fear, you had no respect. For Viv, winning respect on the hard streets of the North-East was possible largely because he had been a champion amateur boxer.

Although constantly in the midst of urban battle, Viv had a carefree way of living and was generous to good causes. The deprived community he came from gave him a lifelong respect for the poor. His benevolence to local charities and schemes to keep kids away from drugs and crime was well known. Indeed, any patch that Viv was protecting was guaranteed to be free of both scourges. To many he was the fourth emergency service; even the police would unofficially recommend him to those with problems.

As time progressed, Viv became entangled in the chaotic quagmire of disorganised crime and was catapulted to the next square on the chessboard of life. Thanks to his size and boxing skills, he could easily ward off any potential upstarts and soon became known for his ability to handle trouble. Others, though, seized on this as an insurance policy and would have Viv around as protection, exploiting his initial naivety to further their own goals.

Soon Viv was taken under the wing of a mentor, a leading underworld figure, who advised his protégé what line to pursue. But it seems Viv had his own ideas. His weakness was for gambling and women. Live hard and play hard, for tomorrow I may be dead, was his philosophy.

During his meteoric rise, Viv was noticed by those higher up the underworld food chain. He knew that he would be asked to enforce some difficult situations and that now he was in the big league he had to beef up his body. He was a lean and mean fighting machine, but that alone doesn't deter troublemakers. Size is what matters. So Viv, insecure about his physique, experimented with steroids and soon ballooned to 18 stone. Now he looked the part of an underworld enforcer, an awesome force to be reckoned with.

Soon Viv was in demand from Tyneside to Tenerife. It looked like money was never going to be a problem and that everyone wanted to be his friend.

Viv had to put a stop to a crime family's drug dealing. But in their eyes he had become too big for his boots and they wanted rid of him at any cost. A plot was hatched to draw him into a fight with another underworld character, but Viv cottoned on to the plan and sidestepped the challenge. The fight never took place because Viv was sure that, no matter what the outcome of the clash, he would be murdered anyway.

When a masked gang attacked Viv's girlfriend's home in order to taunt him into action, again he refused to be drawn into a web of death.

After news of the other hard man's death swept across the region, Viv felt free to expand his empire, especially now the threat of being drawn into a set-up had passed. His legendary name went before him, but his status made him complacent about the security he once insisted on to ensure he always stayed on top. Confrontations with other criminals made him a target for their vengeance and it was only a matter of time before he would be assassinated. Viv had parked his car to visit a pub, when his fate was sealed by a gunman hiding in the darkened lane.

Ultimately, it was Viv's dedication to keeping the streets safe that led to his downfall. The territory he controlled was highly desirable to powerful figures in the drugs world, but all the while he was alive his dominance ensured they could never hope to move in and ply their trade. Viv's gangland assassination sent shock waves throughout the local community and the criminal world. The media storm that ensued grossly distorted the facts about the man, making him out to be a drug boss at the top of a multi-million-pound criminal empire. Nothing could have been further from the truth.

With the passing of the years, the name of Viv Graham still echoes enough to make people stop and think about him. This is his story.

> The Moving Finger writes; and, having writ,
> Moves on: nor all thy Piety nor Wit
> Shall lure it back to cancel half a Line,
> Nor all thy Tears wash out a Word of it.

> *The Rubaiyat of Omar Khayyam*

1

GUNNING FOR VIV
AT SANTINO'S

Viv was no stranger to fighting it out hand to hand. 'I don't need guns,' he would blast, holding up his huge fists. Such he-man heroics are laughed at today, only a decade after his death, but an incident in a restaurant in Newcastle shows the strength of his claim.

On 22 August 1988, Robert Bell, a close friend of Viv, was to encounter a gunman in the city's heaving Bigg Market area of what is classed as one of the party capitals of the world. Bell was involved in some trouble when a fight broke out in the restaurant. About a dozen people took part in a fracas that led to three arrests by police for drunkenness and public-order offences. It was alleged that one of the people involved in the trouble was 'Gentleman' Peter Donnelly, 24, who had got into a fight with Bell over a woman. Another story alleged that Bell had stepped in to break up an argument that Donnelly was having with one of Bell's friends and Bell got the better of Donnelly. It was said that the scene was witnessed by a crowd of bystanders and the police were called to break up the fight.

Donnelly went home and changed his bloody clothes. Maybe he intended to stay there but changed his mind because he felt the need to keep face over the clash he had had with Bell. When your macho image is spoiled, it has to be won back if it is important to you. Some people might have said, let it drop, it's not worth it, and left it at that. The fight had ended and should have been left at that, but instead retribution was sought. Donnelly may have taken a disliking to being outnumbered and thought it unfair of Bell to pile into someone else's fight and take sides, so giving that person an unfair advantage over him.

Weapons were brought into play to even up the situation. Bell was a formidable opponent for anyone by virtue of his size and power. Donnelly was no match against this, yet he was of a mind to get even somehow.

In a meeting I had with Peter Donnelly some years ago (which was not in connection with this book), he told me that, before the confrontation with Bell, Viv had called at Donnelly's home. There, for one reason or another, trouble had started and Viv had lost control, humiliating Donnelly by giving him a hiding in front of his family.

Donnelly told me that, in retaliation, later that day he set off with a gun and found Viv in a restaurant in Newcastle city centre. He pulled the trigger to shoot him, but the gun failed to go off. Donnelly told me this story without prompting. Before I had met him, some people had said to me that he was an animal. How far from the truth this was. Towards me, he acted with the gentlemanly conduct of a cavalry officer. Whether or not he was telling me the truth, he seemed to be genuinely helpful as far as the main issue that I wanted to talk to him about was concerned. Judging by his demeanour, Donnelly was clearly not a person to be easily rattled, whatever might happen to him.

It's anyone's guess what could have made him flip on the night he is alleged to have returned to the restaurant in Cloth Market after the earlier incident there, armed with a gun and a carving knife. What could made him so mad that he seemingly threw caution to the wind in carrying out the alleged violent attack, apparently unconcerned whether Bell was killed? His mental stability had been assaulted and he was really pissed off at Bell. Obviously I cannot ask Donnelly what caused him to act in this way as he was acquitted of a lot of charges owing to lack of evidence and has no wish to incriminate himself, and thus leave himself open to fresh charges.

It is further alleged that Donnelly had an accomplice with him who was never identified when he returned to Cloth Market looking for Bell just after midnight. Bell was in Santino's, sitting at a table with Viv and others when violence flared up. Donnelly's accomplice stayed at the front of the restaurant, armed with a large knife, while Donnelly walked in and went towards Bell. Guests thought the place was about to be robbed by a pair of villains.

Bell, though, later admitted that he knew Donnelly was coming for him. Even so, it must have been a sobering experience to be confronted by Donnelly pointing a 12-bore shotgun at his face at close range.

Out of nowhere, a massive fist moved faster than an eye could blink and took hold of the weapon, and a powerful arm twisted it from Donnelly's grasp like taking candy from a baby. To do this must have taken a split-second decision on Viv's part, and here the rapid reactions he had learned as a boxer were brought into play. Viv detested the use of weapons in a fight, although this was easy for him to profess, given his pugilistic abilities. No doubt what caused him to grab the gun was his anger that such effrontery should take place in view of his fellow late-night diners.

Smashing the shotgun off a nearby wall, Viv caught sight of the glint of metal. All hell broke loose as the unknown man who had been standing guard dashed across the restaurant brandishing his knife. As the knifeman pointed the cold steel at the stomach of Bell's younger brother, 21-year-old Ian, someone brought a chair crashing down over the assailant's head, sending him sprawling across the ground.

During the melee, Bell and Donnelly somehow ended up in the alley behind the restaurant. In the ensuing fight, Bell, it seemed at the time, was mortally wounded from being stabbed in the shoulder and heart.

The heart being a pump, when punctured it still pumps, and Bell's forced blood out through the puncture wound like a fountain of Italian red wine. By now, Viv was on hand a second time, throwing a punch that was to break Donnelly's jaw. Even in the dimly lit alley, Viv could see the blood gushing out of his friend's body and was so incensed that he lost control, lifted a beer keg and smashed it off Donnelly's body. Then he took off his top and stemmed the blood flowing from Bell's wounds while they waited for an ambulance.

Viv had saved his friend's life, as Bell would have been a dead man for sure if Viv had not been there. First, Viv had snatched the gun from Donnelly, then he had set about him, stopping him from completing the job, and finally he had staunched the flow of Bell's blood. (How ironic that, years later outside a pub, Viv would be held in the arms of fellow troubleshooter Terry Scott as his own lifeblood drained from fatal gunshot wounds.)

For Viv's heroics there would be no bravery award, nor any recognition of his valiant action. Had it been anyone else, the hero would have ended up festooned with medals and plastered all over the front page of the local paper, but because Viv was a known hard man it did not count.

It was accepted that for Viv it was all in a day's work to be involved in this sort of incident. But, just because he was a powerful man and his exterior never cracked in public, it did not mean he was not an ordinary human capable of emotion. The ordeal must have been just as daunting for him as it would have been for anyone else. The only, but crucial, difference was that his disciplined boxer's mind had allowed him to react quickly and rescue a dangerous situation.

Later Bell was to recollect that four men had entered Santino's with guns to get them. This may have been bending the truth somewhat – but so what! The man deserved some leeway, considering his injuries, which put him in a critical condition such that at times it was touch and go whether he would pull through. Also, as a consequence of being in hospital, he lost his building business.

The strict underworld code of keeping shtum about such incidents meant nothing to Viv. His close friend was lying at death's door and he knew the potential killer, so he made a statement to the police, aware that this could be a murder case if Bell did not last the night.

Eventually Bell made a statement, as did his brother Ian. In their statements, they named Donnelly as the attacker. Donnelly was remanded to prison to await trial and it has been alleged by one of his associates that an offer of some

£15,000 was offered to Bell not to give evidence against Donnelly in the forthcoming trial. (Author's note: I must point out that this is only an allegation and not to be accepted as fact, but readers are advised to reach their own conclusions after considering the events that followed this alleged deal.)

Bell is alleged to have accepted the offer as he was now on the road to recovery after being at death's door, although it was a long road and that night remains in his waking thoughts and his nightmares. Certainly, £15,000 would have softened the blow that the loss of his business had caused him.

The charges that were put to Donnelly were: attempted murder, wounding with intent, possessing a firearm without a certificate, having a firearm with intent to endanger life and having a firearm in a public place. If found guilty, he was sure to be looking at 15–20 years in prison, if not a life sentence.

After naming Donnelly as his attacker, Bell had a sudden attack of post-traumatic amnesia; he could not remember what had happened or recall who had attacked him. This amnesia thing was contagious, as it also caused memory loss in Ian Bell, who said he was unable to identify the man with the shotgun or the knifeman.

When the case came to trial, during cross-examination, just as the Bells had suffered an attack of amnesia, so Viv too had no recollection of the identities of the attackers. Under oath, he said that he had lied to the police about the identity of a man he had named in a statement he made to the police at the time of the incident.

This must have been music to the ears of Peter Donnelly, who had pleaded 'not guilty' and was standing in the dock with his fingers crossed.

Regardless of the amount of money that allegedly was going to be paid by Donnelly to Bell, it was highly unlikely that Viv would reveal the attacker's identity to the court. It was a different matter to give evidence in a murder hearing, but Bell had recovered from the stabbing and Viv, with his reputation to think of, naturally did not want to become known as a grass. (Nevertheless, after his death, he was accused of being a police informant.)

Not surprisingly, the jury found Donnelly not guilty of attempted murder and he was acquitted of this charge. Cleared also of the remaining charges, Donnelly was to walk free from court.

There, you might think, the story ends; not just yet, though. The romantic notion of honour among thieves is as far from the truth as the cliché that promiscuity is rife among eunuchs. The sweetener of £15,000 that was allegedly to have been paid to Bell was now in Donnelly's back pocket as he left the area and went to a travellers' site at Hull, where he stayed for some time, self-exiled. Here, among his own type, he lay low, fearing a reprisal that would have been accepted as fair retaliation since the allegedly promised £15,000 cash had not changed hands. Donnelly had 'cocked out' of the deal.

Some months later, when Donnelly thought things had calmed down, he returned to Newcastle and visited a city-centre pub called the Fish Bar. Out of the blue, Viv appeared. What a sight this must have been to Donnelly! On seeing his nemesis coming towards him, he broke down in tears, asking Viv not to set about him. Viv told him not to worry; he was not going to set about him. He then promptly dispatched the screaming Donnelly from the pub and threw him into a rubbish skip in the street.

At the end of April 1989 Viv was to experience what a gun that did not jam could do, when he and his then best mate, Robin Armstrong, had potshots fired at them from a pump-action shotgun. After they were stalked from the Quayside area of Newcastle to Manhattan's nightclub, a few minutes away in Carliol Street, just after 1.30am, five shots were blasted at them. Later, after Viv's death, a leading underworld figure told me the story as follows: 'Three crackerjacks carried out the attack because one of them had a run-in with Viv at a nightclub door when Viv wouldn't let them in and he decided to get even. That is all there was to it.'

There is no doubt that Viv had become complacent as far as his own security was concerned. A black Nissan had shadowed him, but he did not recognise it when later it pulled up and waited for him to get out the car he was in. The gunman shot out of the Nissan's rear window, safe inside this fast car. That is how frightened they were of Viv's power: they feared that even a pump-action shotgun might not be enough to slow him down, and they weren't taking any chances.

Unlike Viv, Armstrong had his wits about him and could see what was going on. Shouting 'Move!', he dived on Viv, who had his back to the masked gunman, and pulled him to the ground. For this heroic deed, Armstrong paid a price. He was shot in the back while making for Viv and shot at again while lying protectively over the top of him on the ground. An emerging clubber suffered slight facial injuries from the shotgun blast.

The incident was over as fast as it had started. The black Nissan sped off with its occupants packed inside; there was no way these sardines were going to fall out of their protective tin into the hands of Viv. In time-honoured style, the car was dumped and torched a mile away, with no identification plates on it.

Within hours, Armstrong and the slightly injured man were discharged from hospital; Armstrong, though in pain, was still mobile. Viv had survived this attempted murder, but only just. This incident underlines an important weakness in his outlook: he was not spatially aware of the danger that lurked around him. He took too much for granted, a habit that may have stemmed from his upbringing in a rural environment where things could be trusted to go pretty much the same way, day in and day out.

By contrast, Armstrong, huge as he was, had moved so quickly that it seemed he was acting on instinct. In fact, most able-bodied city dwellers have this ability, even if it involves just the simple action of jumping out of the way of a car or running across a busy road. In city people such reactions are a conditioned reflex.

Nevertheless, nobody dared to get too close to Viv; if they wanted to kill him, they couldn't take any risks. The man's raw physical power meant he might still be able to get them even after being shot, so they had to be able to avoid his landing a blow on them. It was for this reason that they had chosen to carry out their attack from a speedy car.

A member of the criminal fraternity claimed that one of the men involved in the shooting had been party to the vicious burglary of a 90-year-old man's home. The elderly victim, Thomas Hall, was tied up and left for a day with the heating turned off, before being found nearly dead. This callous act – Mr Hall died a short while after he was hospitalised– echoes the cowardliness of shooting at a man's back from a vehicle.

In May 1998, Gary Thompson, 31, was charged with the

murder of Thomas Hall the previous November. Eleven others had various related charges against them. Based on underworld information of the highest calibre, it has been alleged that Thompson is the gunman who shot at Viv and Robin Armstrong from the Nissan nine years earlier. It is alleged also that, after a run-in with Viv, he simply set out to even the score.

Found guilty of the drug-crazed murder of the 90-year-old war veteran Thomas Hall, Gary Thompson appealed against his conviction in July 2000. His bid failed.

When their paths had crossed, back at the end of the 1980s, Viv was already on his way to becoming a sought-after man – even if it was by gunmen.

2

SHOWTIME AT HOBO'S

Viv was turning into a well-honed fighting machine, but although he was a mean, lean weight and fast with his fists, he was, like others, tempted to dabble with steroids. Unlike many others, he was brave enough to admit that he was using them.

Within the space of a few days in the spring of 1989, Viv had been a witness at an attempted murder trial and had been shot at by a masked gunman and now here he was in court to face a charge of GBH. The charge stemmed from an incident in February the previous year and now, in May 1989, he was standing in the dock wondering if the storm was going to end. He faced a custodial sentence, but his 'guilty' plea had cut some ice with Judge Angus Stroyan.

Judge Stroyan heard how Carl Wattler was rushed to hospital for emergency surgery to remove a large blood clot at the base of his brain after being found lying unconscious outside Baxters pub in Newcastle. A scan had shown that an operation was needed at once; otherwise, he would have certainly died.

As a consequence of his injury, Carl Wattler was left with nerve damage that caused blurred vision in one eye, headaches and a limp. After the operation he had spent some time in intensive care and had to be put on a ventilator.

The assault occurred after Wattler allegedly failed to finish his drink quickly enough when asked to at closing time. Viv, it was claimed, had acted a bit hastily, but admitted having punched Wattler in the mouth.

What happened after that is unclear. It was said that there was an incident in the street outside Baxters when Viv went to lock the doors. There was certainly some sort of confrontation outside the pub between Viv and Mr Wattler, and it was claimed that a friend of Viv's, who was working the door with him, intervened and struck Wattler's head with an iron bar.

The sentence imposed on Viv was rather light, and he could think himself lucky that he received an 18-month prison term, suspended for 18 months, and was ordered to pay £500 in compensation to his victim.

By all accounts, when Viv hit someone he would use a degree of force proportionate to their size. If they were knocked out, in some cases, he would catch them in mid-fall, before they hit the ground, to prevent further injury.

It seems that when Wattler's life was saved by emergency surgery, it may have sealed Viv's fate. For Wattler would have had to die for it to have had enough effect on Viv's life to make him change his ways. But, because he returned from death's door, this theory was never put to the test. Viv always warned rowdy people three times to behave themselves, and maybe it was this incident that first caused him to do so.

From Baxters, Viv went to work in Cats. Under the Club Doorman Registration Scheme, which was brought in later, Viv would have been barred from working the doors because he now had a criminal record. Again, a twist of fate came too late. It might have nipped Viv's impending fame in the bud and changed the course of events; but it did not happen like that.

One of the many good points about Viv was that when he went into battle it was with his fists only. An incident that took place in September 1989 was later to show the region that Viv was not to be messed with. When video footage was eventually shown of an incident in Hobo's nightclub in Newcastle, it was clear that he needed no other weapon to do his talking for him. He did not need a 12-bore or a cutthroat razor to make people listen. He did not threaten to burn your home down if you could not meet a debt he was meant to collect. He did not threaten to petrol bomb your family and home.

Viv, who had no use for weapons in his box of tricks, was respected because of his firmness in handling situations. If you deserved it, you got it, and that was that, finished. He held no grudges. This man did not use a gun to threaten or shoot anyone, nor did he need to use pliers to pull at noses, teeth or toenails.

In September 1989, the doorman responsible for policing admission to Hobo's nightclub in the centre of Newcastle was Stuart Watson, 29. Stephen Sayers, a member of a renowned Newcastle criminal family, had been refused entry to the club by Watson. Looking as sick as a parrot, Sayers and others came across Viv, and a story was spun about Stu Watson breaking the jaws of 'a couple of young 'uns', how he stopped them going into Hobo's and how he had said he did 'not care who Viv Graham was'. The one who did all the talking was Stephen Sayers, and with Davie Lancaster and Rob Armstrong there, it looked like Stu Watson was about to get a really good going-over.

The bloodthirsty rabble made their way to Hobo's, where Stu was standing inside the door. Viv went up to him and, after words were exchanged, it was obvious that Stu did not want any trouble, especially with a rogues' gallery like them around. (Viv, Lancaster and Armstrong were the main men, built for action, and along for the ride were Stephen Sayers, Alan 'Fish' Tams and John Thompson.)

When Viv threw some punches, Stu could only raise his hands in a flat-palmed way to defend himself. Anyone would have done the same with guys like that standing around wanting his blood.

Since then Stu Watson has spoken of the brutal attack on him, of the circumstances surrounding the build-up to it and why he could not retaliate. Even so, he had managed to humiliate Viv by taking his best shots while not returning any and not being floored.

Before the incident, Stu and Viv had fallen out. Stu explains: 'It went back further than that with Viv and me. We had a bit of a do down at Julie's nightclub about 18 months before the Hobo's incident. He, Viv, comes in and a few words were exchanged. I didn't know he was in the building. He come across and put his arm across my shoulder in a friendly sort of way and he said, "You're [John] Jobie's pal?"

'I replied, "Yes," and he gave me a sly uppercut on the chin.

'I've still got a scar on my chin even now after all these years. He didn't drop me. I pushed him off and we had a bit of argy-bargy and Rob Armstrong and a couple of other kids were with him. We burst out on to the street and a few words were exchanged. We were going to have a fight up the back lane, but then all the doormen on the Quayside were Viv's mates and more or less worked for him down there, and the trouble dispersed.

'It never stopped at that, though, and I was supposed to meet him up at the Bridle Path pub up at Whickham [near the Metro Centre shopping complex] the next day, Sunday.

'He ended up actually shaking my hand after the set-to on the Saturday night and said, "I'd like you to come in with me," and as he shook hands with me he said, "I'd like to get all this sorted out."

'I met with a few of the lads down at Dunston [just south of the Tyne] and it was me and a lad called Stephen Vaughan, who used to be a good friend of mine, and I went up to Whickham to meet Viv and Armstrong and they never turned up, so that was that.

'A while after that, Cecil and Reg Levy offered me to do the door at Hobo's. Cecil asked, "Will you do the door?" He went on to say that he didn't want the likes of Viv Graham or the Sayers in the place. I said I would keep them out.

'So the first couple of nights nothing was said, but word got back to me that a few of them were running around the town and were coming up to see me. I said to a few of the lads on the door at the time, Joe Quince, Stephen "Flash" Gordon and a few other lads who were working with me, "Don't let them in the door. If they come to the door, give me a shout. I'm inside and I'll come and sort it out."

'One of the doormen come and told me that Viv and his team were at the door. I snapped, "At the door!"

'So when I went in they said that Viv wasn't at the door

but actually in the foyer of the club. "Who's let the fuckers in?" I asked.

'So I went straight out to the foyer and I went to the door and they were standing in the corner and as I went through the door I actually walked past them. Again I demanded, "Who's let these in?"

'A voice behind me, Viv's, barked, "Watson!"

'I turned around and he gave me a left hand straight away and I reeled back and the rest of them, five or six of them, stood around me and were goading Viv: "Go on, Viv, do him! Kill him, kill him! Do him!"

'I knew two or three of them were blade merchants. I knew they'd be tooled up. Soon as he hit me I knew he hadn't done anything with me. I was going to have a shot, but I could see I was in a no-win situation with him, especially when the doormen who were supposed to be standing with me fucked off out of the door. They dropped me like a hot pebble. My girlfriend was there and she could be heard squealing in the background – this was on the CCTV footage that was subsequently played in the courtroom at Viv's trial for the assault on me. One of the doormen had a hold of her – she wanted to intervene herself. I'm married to her now.

'Viv is still giving it to me, batting me, and at the finish we burst into the club itself and he still couldn't put me on my arse. By this time Viv was running out of puff and he pleads to me, "Go down! Go down, man!"

'The others who were with Viv had kicked open the fire-exit doors by this time and everybody had made a big space for them and they were saying to him, "Get him outside, we'll kill him!"

'Viv was still shouting at me, "Go down! Go down!"

'I believe Viv was more concerned at what was going to

happen because he didn't have the arse for it, because if they'd have killed me or stuck me, then he was in the shit and he knew it. I didn't go down, though. I kept a hold of the spiral staircase, he didn't hurt me, but they were like a pack of dogs and jumped in and started punching and kicking me.

'Viv stopped it, and in wide-eyed disbelief he was shouting, "He's had enough. He's had enough! That's it!"

'I was all cut and Viv was looking worried.

'I said, "Is that it, then? Are you finished?"

'My wife, Sharon, was crying her eyes out. I consoled her: "I'm all right, they haven't hurt me. I'm all right."

'I went to the toilet to clean my face up, got in the car and went to hospital to have a few stitches put in. That happened on the Friday or Saturday night. By the Monday, I was back at work. The instigator of the attack was Davie Lancaster ... he's a little man with a big mouth and he likes to throw fuel on the fire. I've never professed to be anybody; I'm just a man off the streets.

'I was one who wouldn't bow down to them. If I was given a job to do and they asked me to do a job and I was being paid to do that job, then I did the job and if they didn't want them in the club, then I'd keep them out. If you're being paid to do the job, then you do the job. If you cannot, then they'll just get somebody else to do it.

'After that I was arrested three times for perverting the course of justice because I had a meeting with John Sayers, which the police knew about. And he started out by telling me that I should do this and do that. He didn't ask me at first.

'I said, "You don't tell me to do nothing, ask me and then we might get somewhere, but don't tell me." Dodgy Ray Hewitson was there at the meeting.

'What happened on the night of the fight was there were three or four undercover police in Hobo's and, when Viv and the others were up in court for the fight, the police were asked about when they were supposed to intervene in any sort of violence. They said that they had orders from the top saying that they didn't have to intervene at all; they had to let it go to see what happened. That's why you get people turning against the police, full stop – because they were using me. They were hoping I was going to get killed or if I was stabbed up, then they had to do nothing! Their orders were "not to intervene at any time".

'I said to the police that it was me who threw the first punch but, of course, it was on video and they weren't having any of it. I made an affidavit saying I'd started the fight. The police asked me if they owed me anything.

'I said, "You owe me fuck all, I owe you nothing and you owe me fuck all. I want nothing off you."'

[Watson refused to allow his medical records to be used in court and did not give evidence at the court hearing when Viv and his team faced charges for assault. It can also be said that the police were keen to make a case of it all.]

'When Viv comes home on a home leave from his three-year sentence he had a big party. I went down – the whole lot of them were there – and I went down and showed my face.

'Dodgy Ray said, "He's out, do you want to break the ice?"

'I replied, "I'm not bothered about going down."

'They were all in Macey's nightclub and I went down. As soon as I walked in the front doors you could have heard a pin drop.

'After that Viv and me were working together at Rockshots nightclub. Dodgy Ray was the go-between for Viv and me. Every time Viv and me were there, you could cut the atmosphere with a knife. I could tell that Viv was dubious of me and wasn't sure if he could take my shots or not and it was always the case where he was always doubtful and you could feel the atmosphere there all the time. I knew from day one that it wasn't going to work, me and him working together, because he just couldn't let things go at that and he wasn't sure what would've happened if we did have a proper fight.

'So when we're working Rockshots together he was getting X amount of pounds and I'm getting X amount of pounds and he was coming in once every two weeks, three weeks, and I was there like a mug standing on the door and he's getting the same money as me for not being there. So they in the club say they want Newcastle's West End lot kept out because they were making a nuisance of themselves and some of them were doing what they wanted.

'So I said on the Thursday, "Right, no more West End in" to the lads at the door. I said, "If any names come in, then I'm inside. Come and tell me and then I'll come out and tell them that they cannot come in." I went on to say, "You lads on the doors don't get paid enough for that, that's my job."

'They were kept out good style and not one of them got in. Viv was still half pally with the West End lot at the time but he said all right to the club's demands of keeping them out. It was getting to the point that I was fighting nearly every other day on the door and I was getting threats to kill me: "You're going to get shot" and all the usual shite.

'Then Viv was away for six weeks and I still had his money and then Dodgy Ray said, "Viv wants his money!"

'I seethed, "Tell Viv he's not getting his fucking money!"

'He bleated, "He's not going to be happy!"

'I fumed, "Tell him I'm not happy, me doing his fucking

work and he's getting the same money. Tell him he's not getting it!"

'Apprehensively, he says, "You know what he'll be like."

'I said, "I don't give a fuck, he's not getting it. I'm not going to do his job on top of mine. I couldn't give a fuck what he says!"

'Dodgy Ray went to see Viv and he half accepted what I'd said and he told Dodgy Ray, "Tell him he can keep the cunt for his fucking self."

'So I pulled a few more lads in rather than me keep his money. I felt a little bit more secure and I had some decent lads with me.

'Viv was up at Madison's, say, three or four times a year or so and he'd phone Rockshots up and he'd say to me, "People are telling me I can't fucking do you."

'I asked, "Who's telling you this?"

'He'd reply, "People told me that."

'"Well, who the fuck is it?" I'd reply.

'He's giving it the big one on the phone, so I cracked. "Who's saying this?"

'It turned out it was Mackem Tommy, who used to work for me, then he went to work for Viv up at Madison's nightclub.

'Viv was still on the phone, saying, "He told me I didn't drop you."

'I said to him, "Well, you didn't fucking drop me!"

'"I'll tell you what, I'm going to come down," was what he said.

'I told him to come down but "there's just going to be trouble, but I'll tell you what I'll do, I'm going to come to your house tomorrow."

'I went to his house with Geoff Brown because Geoff knew where he lived. I went there, knocked on the door, he answered all apologetic and shaking my hand and that.

'I asked, "What the fuck's the matter with you? If you're going to listen to people, then we're going to be at each other's throats all the time."

'Viv said, "Aye, I know. I know."

'We were once in Rockshots when we used to work together and Dodgy Ray come across and he says, "Stu, Viv wants you to go over and knock that kid out."

'I retorted, "Viv wants me to go and do what?" I wasn't doing Viv's dirty work, so I blasted, "Tell fucking Viv to do it himself. I'm not his fucking monkey. Tell him to fucking do it!"

'He must have thought I was going to work for him. I didn't work *for* anyone, I worked *with* them.'

Stu went on to tell of a further confrontation he had with Viv: 'I was at the gym with a friend of mine called Todd when Viv come in and he said that he wanted to see me outside. Viv voiced his demands to me as we're standing at the front of the gym, "I want £15,000 off you or Adrian." He wanted this for his part in keeping trouble out of Rockshots.

'I said, "You're getting nothing out of me!"

'This was two years after he had left Rockshots; he was short of money and he was a gambler. He would see that you were doing half all right and wanted some of it.

'Todd came out of the gym and Viv yelled at him, "What are you fucking coming out for?"

'Viv went to throw a punch at Todd and I grabbed a hold of Viv when he went forward to punch him and pulled him back and he threatened me, "Don't you fucking jump on my back!"

'I was seeing red. "Jump on your back! I haven't jumped on your fucking back, it's got fuck all to do with him, it's between me and you."

'Viv then bawled, "Get round the fucking back with me!"

'I told him, "Anything you've got to do with me, you can do round the front. I'm going round no back. I don't know who the fuck's round there."

'"I want 15 grand off you," Viv demanded.

'I angrily retorted, "You're getting fuck all off me. I'll ask Adrian about it and, if Adrian doesn't know anything about it, then you're getting fuck all."

'I saw Adrian and said to him, "Tell Viv he's getting fuck all. I'm standing by you."

'At that time the club was in trouble anyway – it had lost its drinks licence – and he wanted 15 grand out of a club that wasn't making anything.

'Then it was a couple of nights after that we went down to the Lion pub [a haunt of the hard-man fraternity, in Felling, Gateshead] and it was a Bank Holiday Monday. He was coming out of the Lion as we were going in and there was a little bit of animosity, you could feel it, and we were having a bit of eye-to-eye.

'Viv said, "Are you all right?"

'I went, "Aye, I'm all right."

'Later on he left a message that he was coming back that night and he was going to come up to the nearby Malting House pub.

'So we're sitting up at the Malting House and I said to the Hammer [Stephen Eastland], Geoff [Brown] and Terry Mitchell, "If he comes in, then let me and him fucking get it on and see what the fucking outcome is. I'm sick of all this shite."

'And he, Viv, was in a bar [the Lion] about 50 yards away and he never come up. He was threatening he was going to come up, but he never. It was a stand-off all the time, I wish it had got off the ground but it didn't.'

Years down the road from all of that mayhem, Stu Watson has been through the mill and fought back and cleared his name at a massive three-week trial at Newcastle Crown Court in March 2005. Accused of being the Mr Big behind a prostitution ring in the North-East, he faced nine charges.

The prosecution alleged that Watson had been the brains behind a team of helpers who ran brothels, charging prostitutes between £50 and £200 a day to work there. After three weeks, Judge John Milford halted the trial and instructed the jury to clear Watson of all charges. The trial was always doomed to failure, given the police's poor track record in cases like this. A similar trial had collapsed years earlier. A civilian worker employed by a local police force faced charges of employing escorts but the escorts would not testify against him as this would break their anonymity and most were just ordinary housewives.

In the Watson case it was alleged that lone call-girls were threatened in order to force them into the business and call-girls from Thailand were brought to the North-East to help diversify the culture of prostitution and so advance the business.

One of the gang, Graham Davie, 34, of Jesmond, Newcastle, admitted to being second in command and was an associate of the violent Tyneside pimp and rapist 'Turbo' Tommy Hay, who was jailed for 11 years in December 2003 for being part of a separate ring after he turned prosecution witness against Graham Brown, formerly a PC with Northumbria Police. 'Turbo' Tommy revealed how he obtained data-protected information from the Northumbria force's computer by supplying girls in exchange for it.

At the trial Davie pleaded guilty to offences committed between March 1999 and October 2002: two counts of living off the earnings of prostitutes, one of living off the earnings of a named prostitute and one of ABH. He was sentenced to three and a half years and given an extra 12 months for a previous unexpired sentence for drug offences.

Now Watson hopes to get back to his life of running his pub business after being on remand in prison for many months. He said, 'I think it's hard for the community around me, especially the council and the police. I took the kids from the school across the road a number of years ago to see a pantomime because they couldn't raise the money.

'They can't understand how a man can change, but give a dog a bad name and it sticks. I've got three pubs and none of them have a drugs problem. No one is allowed to smoke joints in them and that was made clear from day one. I'm not going to give the police that chance to come down on me again.'

In the incident at Hobo's, Watson had very little option but to go along with it and try to ride out some of the punches. It was the early hours of the morning and there were patrons in the club who had to take cover from what must have looked like General Custer's last stand. Watson was hit at least 20 times in the head by Viv, but he did not go down. Talk about being able to take a punch! This man had a jaw of concrete, and it must have been embarrassing to those six men who could not put him down. Even Viv's father said, 'Six pensioners could have done more damage.'

That night Viv took to throwing Stu Watson about, which looked far worse than it actually was. Anyone who viewed the unedited version of the video footage of the fight that was recorded by the club's CCTV system, as I did, would have seen something totally different from what was shown on TV news programmes.

The tuxedo that Watson was wearing was too big around his waist, as having a large chest – 50 inches in his case – usually means putting up with jackets that have an overgenerous waist size. It looked like he was being rag-dolled about, but in fact a lot of the movement came from the loose-fitting jacket.

When Viv had stunned Watson enough, the vultures came in for the kill, kicking at him, knowing they were safe in having Viv's protection should anything go wrong. But Watson still would not go down. It was like a scene from a *Rocky* movie and plenty of claret to go along with it, though Watson's was the only blood drawn. To give Viv some credit, he only used his hands as weapons. Had an attack on Watson been made by some of the others, he could have expected something worse than fists and feet.

No one deserved the public humiliation that Watson was eventually to suffer when, following Viv's murder, the edited version of the assault at Hobo's was shown in news programmes all over the North-East. To viewers it must have seemed like a massacre, and perhaps it should never have been shown, as they saw only one side of Viv and this has remained etched on their memories.

It's true that there was no chivalry on Viv's part in his unprovoked attack on Watson, no code of conduct or self-discipline. He had the buttons on his back pressed and he was pointed in Watson's direction and let go of like a giant toy. Viv had been told a pack of lies and he was acting on them. He believed every word that was told to him.

To have a man like Viv in your power would be a real ego boost and no one would dare mess with you when he was available to do your bidding. Viv was slow to learn, but this was what he had to put up with. David Lancaster, who was experienced in the ways of the big city, should have known better, but even these lesser mortals controlled Viv.

In court it was alleged that two undercover police officers from Tadcaster, a male and a female, were in Hobo's on surveillance duty and witnessed some of the fight but let it go on, even when a spiked weapon was produced by one of the underlings. Did Watson know of their presence? It is doubtful, as it was a covert police operation and was not likely to be telegraphed to anyone. While Watson was being knocked into next week, these two police officers sat on their rear ends.

It has been further alleged that a police officer asked for a fee of £30,000 for the video recordings to be handed over to Viv and his associates. This assertion, of course, gives another twist to the whole affair but must be accepted as an allegation and not fact.

The gang appeared in court in July 1990, all charged with violent disorder and wounding Watson. The trial lasted for two weeks, five of the six having struck a deal with the prosecution to accept a lesser charge of unlawful wounding. But, whatever the charge was dropped to, it was not going to make any difference to the length of prison sentence each man would serve. Judge Mary MacMurray had viewed the video and ultimately it was a case of dishing out the sentences.

The six men received a total of 14 years and two months' imprisonment: David Lancaster, Robin Armstrong, Stephen Sayers and Alan Tams were each to get two and a half years in prison. Viv received a three-year sentence and the remainder of his outstanding suspended sentence received for his attack on Carl Wattler, ten months, was to run concurrently with it.

Finally, the case of John Thompson was considered. The police apparently had some difficulty catching this man. He was charged with a minor offence of causing fear or provocation of violence and was given four months' imprisonment.

The sentences handed down to the six men were not particularly harsh, considering the attack took place in a nightclub, causing guests to fear for their lives. Viv, in particular, was very lucky not to be facing five years behind bars, given his past form for violence.

Stu Watson must be commended for the way he handled the court case. He would not let the prosecution use any of his medical details in connection with the assault and did not himself give evidence in the trial. He did say, however, that he felt that the Regional Crime Squad used him as bait. This seems to be confirmed by the allegation that a member of Viv's family was told by the police that they knew Viv was a good lad and that it was really the others, including the Sayers, that they wanted but, unfortunately, Viv had got himself caught up in the trap.

As a result of this case and his imprisonment, Viv had been through his rites of passage. While in jail he matured and certainly got to know the full extent of the story. There, he had also fallen out with his pal Rob Armstrong, although this rift was eventually to be patched up.

Like most things that get broken, though, it was not the same when mended. Viv's outlook on life had developed and he kicked into touch a lot of past associates who had used him. He knew what direction he was going in after his time in prison was served.

3

MURDER ON THE
DANCE FLOOR

Viv had learned his lesson in mixing with the big fish of Newcastle's underworld. John Henry Sayers was worlds away from the rest of his family in terms of what he was capable of. The older brother of Michael and Stephen, he was a methodical planner, meticulous, drug-free and fit – all the requirements of a successful planner of robberies. A family man from the Heaton area of Newcastle, John Henry was well liked, and for all the right reasons.

It was alleged that, a short while after Viv was released from prison for his attack on Stuart Watson, he had run Michael Sayers out of a Newcastle nightclub where Sayers was allegedly selling drugs. It was suggested that Viv and Sayers respected each other's territory and that maybe Viv thought in retrospect that he had been wrong to handle Sayers that way.

An underworld source revealed what happened that night:

'He [Viv] just looked at him [Sayers] and went running across and he [Sayers] was going, "Argh! Viv, divent, divent" and he chased him out through the nightclub door.

'Viv went out after him. I followed and said, "Howway, man. Come back in."

'And he [Viv] was like, "Ohgh!"

'And he [Sayers] was going, "Please, please, please, divent," and it calmed down.

'Viv came back in and Sayers slumped off with a minor pasting.'

Then there are the Tams family, from the West End of Newcastle, who go back some years in the history of local criminality but have not featured prominently in crime for some while. Alan 'Fish' Tams, along with Stephen Sayers and David Lancaster, were arrested on the holiday island of Tenerife, off Africa's Atlantic coast, in April 1989. They were caught in possession of Ecstasy tablets and 'tac' (dope).

They had not even got out of Reina Sofia Airport before they were searched by security staff and subsequently detained in the not-too-uncomfortable Granadilla Detention Centre. Obviously they had brought their drug ration with them to see them through their holiday.

Being a family member means that there is always someone to protect your interests or take retribution against anyone trying it on. That was the fundamental difference between these people and Viv. He was a loner; he did not need anyone to fight his battles for him. But maybe that was a problem, because, although Viv had associates and people he could call on, who was there that was as sincere about the things he did as a close family member would be? He was a lone tiger in a jungle, more powerful than any individual, but he could not fight an organised strike launched against him by men of violence. Viv was brutal, yes, but not brutal beyond redemption.

He was the minders' minder, on call if anything got out of hand, single-handedly policing the bouncers and keeping order. His knowledge of what was really going on in Newcastle was limited to some extent by his being in demand right across the region to organise door-security staff. He had some lieutenants on call but most often their role was purely cosmetic. His word was the law in a city that the police had lost control of, albeit temporarily. And even though, towards the end of his life, he concentrated his services away from the centre of Newcastle, he still knew what the particular groups who operated in the heart of the city were up to.

In the early days of his career Viv was hired muscle, along with others, for the Sayers family, but eventually flew solo after coming out of prison in 1992. Viv was the Lone Ranger in a town gone crazy.

Like every other year, Christmas Eve 1989 was a time for celebration – but not for a local woman called Penny Laing. That evening Penny was one of 1,500 revellers crowded into Newcastle's Studio nightclub. Along with her childhood sweetheart, David Storey, and two other friends from the Northumberland village of Annitsford, she was eager to enjoy a celebratory night out. The four of them had to force their way through the crowd to the bar. While pushing through the crowd, it seems that Penny may have been sexually assaulted by a man who briefly caught her attention. In this overcrowded club, wandering hands were a literal pain in the arse for every respectable young woman. Viv detested this sort of behaviour and would take any culprit to task. Unfortunately, he wasn't in the club that evening, otherwise he might have prevented what happened to Penny, although in such a jam-packed venue even his trained eye might have failed to spot it.

Naturally, Penny felt she had to do something about this affront and in classic style she slapped the offender across the face. The man, who was in the company of two blonde women, had a glass in his hand and struck out at her with it – just once.

Nineteen-year-old Penny slumped to the floor, dying from a terrible wound. Deterring this sort of brutality was what Viv was all about: making the city a safer place to be in, a place where you could take your woman out without fear of some divvy abusing, let alone killing, her.

David Storey chased after the attacker, who was seen to be pulled away by the two blonde women, caught up with him at some stairs in the club and threw some blows at him as best he could. The man, who had short, dark hair, left the club quickly and got away in a taxi.

Detective Superintendent John May, who was in charge of the murder inquiry, was appalled at the needless waste of life brought about by a cowardly thug. But investigation of the vicious and unwarranted attack was met with a wall of silence. No one wanted to come forward with information, even though it was the act of a coward against a defenceless young woman who had her whole life ahead of her. It was rumoured that the attacker was known to other clubbers, but still no one came forward to help, until an anonymous telephone call made by a female at 7pm on Christmas Day.

By this time, a young man had been put on a plane bound for the USA by his father. The man was Stephen Craven, 25, unemployed, from Heaton. Running away from this situation was only to strengthen the eventual prosecution case against him for the murder of Penny Laing.

The appalling nature of the attack on Penny had caused some people to feel guilt about withholding information and the wall of silence had shattered. Soon the beans were spilling all over the place, with information coming in thick and fast about the attacker's identity.

Stephen Craven was arrested a few days later as he arrived at Heathrow Airport on a flight from America. He was remanded in custody, where eventually he met Viv, who was serving his 'three stretch' for the attack on Hobo's club doorman Stuart Watson. Craven told Viv that he had not been involved in Penny's murder and that a marine had killed her. This, he said, accounted for the fact that the police were told that a man with short hair with cropped sides had been seen to leave the club in a hurry.

To cut a long story short, Viv believed Craven's story that he had been fitted up. It was in Viv's nature to believe what people were saying and it reflects the sensitive side of a man sometimes accused of being just a hard case. Viv was like an oyster, hard on the outside, but open him up and there was his pearl of a heart. He and Craven became friends while in prison.

On Viv's release on parole, in July 1991, Craven's father approached him, saying that it was not his son who had killed Penny in the nightclub attack. Viv, a believer in justice having to be seen to be done, confronted a doorman who was on duty at the Studio and grabbed him by the lapels, demanding he say who the killer really was. But not even Viv's intervention could change the doorman's mind; he was not shifting from his story that it was Craven.

Viv pursued the marine said to have carried out the attack

and asked him to return to the North-East from London, hand himself in to the police and take what was coming to him. But when Viv visited the police to find out what they knew, he was put straight on a few points that had not been disclosed to the press, and having had the full story told to him in confidence, he relented and let go of the cause.

Stephen Craven was eventually found guilty of the murder of Penny Laing and given a life sentence, although he still insisted on his innocence.

4

PHANTOM FIGHTS

To understand how fundamentally indifferent Viv was to his safety, you have to look at how his opposite number on Teesside fared. You can take the boy out of the city but you can't take the city of the boy, and this highlights the crucial difference between Viv Graham and Lee Duffy. Viv came from the little urban village of Highfield, near Rowlands Gill, south-west of Newcastle, and, even though he tried to make inroads into the underworld scene on Tyneside, he still had some of the village in him. But Duffy, you could put him wherever you wanted and he would survive because of his streetwise instinct.

Although pub enforcer Viv quickly earned a reputation on Tyneside as a hard man with a heart of gold, he was matched by Duffy over on Teesside. Viv took every fight with a pinch of salt. His size and boxing skills made him an excellent insurance policy against the thugs and drug dealers who polluted the pub and club scene. Lee Duffy was running a parallel and equally untenable life on the pub and club circuit of Middlesbrough. Murder, mayhem, drugs, violence and sex were the currency of the crime-ridden underbelly of both areas.

From Land's End to John O'Groats, no city or town is without those who have carved out a name for themselves as true hard men. Down south, London had the Krays and Lenny ('The Guv'nor') McLean; the North-East had Viv and Lee.

Viv's chosen sport of amateur boxing came to an abrupt end when he developed a frozen shoulder, which is how he started out as a doorman in the rural outskirts of Newcastle. Unwittingly, he became immersed in the swamp of disorganised crime and was to pay the ultimate price when the higher echelons of that world decided to knock him off his perch for barring them from his territory.

Lee Duffy, 'the Duffer', was a formidable-looking giant of a man. His presence was felt before he even entered a room, and this attracted the opposite sex as surely as it unsettled his own. He was enjoying the benefits of multiple, tangled relationships with the women of Teesside. On-the-spot sex in pub and club toilets with eager groupies was a regular occurrence and played a role in confirming his dominance over his peers.

Viv, like most champs, had a vice; he betted on anything – dogs, horses, football and fights. (When he didn't know the fighters, he chose his bet by the colour of the boxer's shorts!) He was on a rollercoaster and enjoyed every minute of it, but he just did not open his eyes to where the ride was taking him.

Duffy was on just as hectic a ride with his 'taxing' of drug dealers, along with his 'business' partner, Brian Cockerill, aka the 'Tax Man'. And hitting the local cocaine trade was the Duffer's obsession.

It was Viv's barring of drug dealers from his territory, along with his general hard-man reputation, that attracted the attentions of a notorious crime family from Newcastle's West End who, it was claimed, controlled most of the flow of drugs in the city. At first, they tried to put him on their payroll and even started down the road of befriending him; but his spell in prison made him see sense. It was this dramatic turnaround in Viv's outlook that prompted the shadowy figures of crime to enlist the help of Lee Duffy to defeat him in a winner-takes-all fight.

Viv was changing from a man who wanted to make pubs and clubs safer for everyone to a bully who struck fear into the hearts of the people whom he was supposed to protect.

The Duffer had attempts made on his life after he was classed as the bully of Teesside. A drug dealer ordered a hit on the man no one dared approach head on.

Like Viv with his assault on Stu Watson at Hobo's, the Duffer found that his strength could get him into trouble. When he felled a club doorman with a single punch, the vertebrae in the victim's neck were crushed. The police refused to believe one punch could cause so much damage. Soon both Viv and the Duffer were back in the headlines – Viv for pummelling Watson and the Duffer for breaking the jaw of a man who threw petrol over him while holding a lighter at the ready.

While Viv was in prison, two of his three girlfriends, Anna and Julie, temporarily broke up with him when they found out about each other, leaving only Gillian, who had just given birth to their second son.

The Duffer was in hospital, recovering from gunshot wounds to his leg as a consequence of yet another attempt on his life, when his girlfriend gave birth to his daughter in a different hospital.

Viv was well received by the prison community and enhanced his reputation as an enforcer by quelling a cell-block riot that was about to kick off in the prison chapel. Meanwhile, Tyneside was burning with riots of its own.

As soon as he was a free man again, Viv decided to break all ties with past allies and fly his own flag in the East End of Newcastle. With the help of Peter Connelly, he became a troubleshooter/minder for pubs and clubs, in time expanding his business from a few licensees to quite a little empire.

Just as fast as he raked in the money, he and his fiancèe, Anna, were spending it. Both craved the high life and a bet or two. When it came to blowing cash, they tried to outdo each other – easy come, easy go. Neither of them planned for the future, believing their good fortune would last forever. Viv hid behind the settee when a debt collector called – he'd had £30,000 in a bag the day before, but now it was all gone.

Eventually his concerns began to interfere with those of the West End criminal fraternity. They wanted to expand their thriving drug enterprise, but the anti-drug Viv was in the way, and this is where Duffy came into the equation.

Over on Teesside, Duffy was just as much a thorn in the side of drug pushers as Viv was to the Tyneside drug barons. The Duffer's constant attention to taxing dealers of their drugs and money soon made him a prime target. The drugs he gave away, while the ill-gotten money he showered on his friends.

When the mobsters enlisted Duffy's help to eliminate Viv

in a winner-takes-all bare-knuckle fight, the plan failed – Viv had been warned about an ambush and didn't show up. The daily pressure of the 'big time' started to take its toll on Viv. Loose bowels and frequent headaches were the least of it. More seriously, death threats became the norm for both him and his opposite number on Teesside. 'I'll not see 40,' said Viv, presciently. He had stumbled on to the tiger's back and found he couldn't get off. The Duffer broke down in tears and told his girlfriend he wanted out of that world but didn't know how. Each man was trapped!

Viv and Anna bought a new house just outside Newcastle and he tried to legitimise his pub and club protection business. For the most part his reputation enabled him to sit at home while his delegates dealt with the problems. He spent a lot of time in the Queen's Head pub, near his home.

Duffy, with his girlfriend, Lisa, took on a council house with the intention of 'doing it up' and maybe one day buying it. His reputation, too, was growing and now he had the opportunity to reap the rewards that his name could bring him.

A band of locals took an immediate dislike to Viv. One of them was connected to a West End crime lord, and for a dare, it is claimed, they plotted Viv's murder, adopting the slogan 'Viv no more for '94'.

Teesside's drug circles were united in anger at the Duffer's tax regime and hit after unsuccessful hit was ordered against him. At a secret meeting a small gathering of top dealers planned his death.

Viv and Duffy fiercely resented each other. Each man's name stood for violence and these sworn enemies ran parallel lives as pub and club enforcers, each raging his gangland turf war in a frenzy of brutality and unremitting cruelty. Engaging each other in a vicious organised brawl would have been the ultimate challenge, a clash that would bring bloodshed and carnage. As it turned out, both met a brutal, violent death in other ways and this battle of the titans never took place.

The two men had so much in common:

Both were fond of women and had a constant stream of female admirers.

Both fathered children with a string of women.

Both were family men and doted on their children.

Both predicted their own death in an uncanny way.

Both had a love of boxing, Viv competing and Duffy using his skills on drug dealers' heads.

Both were accused of using weapons to cause an injury to their respective victims. Viv received a suspended sentence while Duffy awaited trial.

Both had a vice. Viv's was gambling and Duffy's was throwing his money away on his friends.

Both used drugs. Viv used steroids and Duffy used a variety of substances, including Class A and Class B drugs, a habit he picked up while serving time.

Both took their girlfriends to Blackpool.

Both had a perverse sense of humour. Viv loved fooling around setting off fire extinguishers. Duffy had his glass trick: he would hold a pint glass and ping the rim against someone's head; the glass would shatter without damaging the person's head. He would do this to a number of people in a pub, then sweep up the mess and give the landlord £50 for the glasses he had smashed.

Both received numerous death threats. Duffy had three attempts made on his life while Viv had one attempt that was called off at the last minute.

Both men's homes were raided by thugs looking for them.

Both were considered the hardest men in their respective areas.

Both went abroad: to Tenerife.

Both started out working the club doors.

Both had a fear: Viv of the dark and Duffy of knives.

Both had more than one girlfriend visit them while in prison.

Both were lone wolves who worked on their own account and bowed down to no other man.

Both were accused, after death, of being drug barons, although neither had ever had a drug conviction.

Both men's local police forces said that no one would be able to replace them and fill the power vacuum, and, if anyone did, they knew what was waiting at the end of it all – which dissuaded everyone from taking up the challenge.

Both men's fiefdoms, Tyneside and Teesside, have seen an increase in illicit drug use since their deaths.

Both men overcame propaganda during their reign.

Both loved a particular sport: Viv became an amateur contender at boxing while Duffy excelled at swimming.

Both wanted to get off the tiger's back but didn't know how.

Both men were in Durham Jail at the same time in 1991.

Both suffered the physical signs of some sort of neurosis. Viv suffered crippling stomach cramps and diarrhoea, and raging headaches. Duffy would break down in private when the odds were against him, telling those he loved that he wanted out of it.

Both were matched against each other. The fight never came off because Viv stayed out of Duffy's way, certain that even if he had won he would have been murdered by those seeking to oust him from his position as Tyneside's top dog.

Both men were held and comforted in the arms of their friends before they died.

Both men's deaths are surrounded in controversy that continues to this day; and both deaths are said to have caused some to celebrate.

Both men's funerals were attended by more than 1,000 mourners.

Both were and are legends. Even in death they can't be matched.

To return to that fight, excited talk of Viv and Duffy slugging it out in one-to-one combat resounded throughout the North-East. In the underworld, some were saying that a fight had been scheduled at the Havana club in Middlesbrough, but Viv hadn't turned up. The rumour about a second organised clash between the two was that Viv, thinking he was going to be shot, again didn't show.

An underworld character from Teesside said, 'No doubt about it, Viv was a very hard man but I don't think Viv would have beat Lee. Something the Sayers might have been worried about was that, if Lee and Viv had got their heads together, then they might have blitzed them clean out of the water. But considering it was going to come off, Lee was permanently up the Mayfair nightclub all the time, constantly up Newcastle, but Viv wasn't down here. There were two arranged fights and Viv didn't turn up at either of them. Viv had a few doors up there and Lee went around and taxed a few of Viv's men. He wanted to put it on Viv's toes because he hadn't turned up.'

Any chance of a fight between Viv and Duffy was curtailed when, at 3.30am on 25 August 1991, outside the Afro-West Indian Centre in Marton Road, Middlesbrough, the Duffer became involved in an argument and was fatally knifed. He died shortly afterwards in the arms of a friend. 'Tell Lisa I love her' were his last words.

VIV GRAHAM

Just as Viv's counterpart in Teesside was as tough as Viv was, so was his opposite number in Sunderland, Ernie Bewick. Many have called Ernie a 'gangland killer' and an 'enforcer', but he is considered by many to be one of the most forgiving men around.

Ernie Bewick's confrontations perhaps numbered as many as Viv Graham's. One that was unleashed upon him had dire results for his opponent. It was 7 December 1997 when convicted drug dealer Tony Waters, 44, died as a result of a fight with Bewick outside the Eastender pub in Sunderland's High Street East.

Waters went looking for Bewick with the aim of doing him damage over an incident that had taken place the previous night between Bewick and two other men in Luciano's restaurant in the town. The fact that Waters so deliberately pursued his man contradicts all those who have maintained since his death that he just wanted a quiet life after his release from prison some four years earlier. It seems that some wish to paint Waters as whiter than white but if that had been the case you would be reading a very different account of his life here.

Waters left behind a family who grieve for him to this day and the time of year of his death, Christmas, makes the pain they feel at the loss of their loved one all the worse. But such sentiments should be put to one side for a moment while we consider the depth of his resentment of Bewick.

Ernie Bewick was and still is anti-drugs. Waters was pro-drugs and well known among the drug fraternity of the North-East. Seeing Bewick as a stumbling block to dealing his drugs in pubs that were under Bewick's charge, he calculated that a successful confrontation might drive him from the area.

Bewick was fully aware of the way Waters was dealing drugs and knew that he was the difference between Sunderland being flooded with drugs and being kept relatively free of them. He was determined that as long as he was in charge of certain pub and club doors it would remain the second. Just as Viv frowned on drugs, so did Bewick, and just as others wanted rid of Viv so that they could deal in his patch on Tyneside, so it seemed to be the same way in Bewick's territory on Wearside. The two men had a lot in common, although Bewick had a slight edge over Graham in his handling of matters and his ability to sense danger.

As for Waters, a terrier-tempered person, he met his untimely end as a direct result of his desire to deal drugs in Sunderland.

Never one to back down from a challenge, Bewick was a man to be admired. In one significant challenge, Viv's mentor, Billy Robinson of Gateshead, another North-East hard man, was to meet Ernie for a 'straightener'. This event illustrates how Viv was becoming tainted by city life.

Bewick himself tells the story, which opens with him working on the door of a nightclub when Robinson and his party turned up: 'That night I was called to the door [of the Blue Monkey, where, according to rumour, Bewick started working because there had been trouble with a well-known dealer selling drugs and because someone had been murdered outside] and they said that Billy Robinson was at the door and he wanted to come in.

'Well, on that particular evening it was the type where everybody had to pay when they came in, so I went up, and I really didn't know Billy at the time and I explained that everybody had to pay to get in. Robinson's henchmen standing beside him said, "Do you know who you're talking to?" and things like that.

'I said, "I'm sorry, you know, but you've got to pay in."

'If anybody had asked me the same thing I'd have said, "Fair enough."

'So then I was being called a "little shit" type of thing and had abuse like that thrown at me, so I said, "Look! You can't come in."

'So he [Robinson] said, "Right, you little thing, get round the corner, you little shit!"

I accepted. "Well, fair enough."

'So then Billy slapped me across the face and I went forward to go into him; he tried to punch me, so I ducked over the punch and gave him a right cross and an uppercut and knocked him out. Then his friends were there, his big henchmen suddenly seemed to deflate, and I said, "Right, get him up and fuck off and don't ever come back here any more!"

'They went, but obviously by then all the talk starts to generate. There were a few scares that they were going to come through team-handed at the door and there was a couple of times we had to prepare for what might have happened.

'Months later I heard rumours that I was going to be set up and different things. One day Keith Bell come knocking on my door trying to go on as though he was a friend and he says, "Look, Billy wants to have a go at you and he wants to see you as soon as possible for a one-to-one."

'I replied, "Fair enough, I'll come now."

'Bell asked, "Well, can you not make it later on tonight? You know where I live; you've been to mine before."

'We went through [to Newcastle] and the whole thing dragged on for a couple of hours while they were talking, so I got something to eat at Keith's. The fight was arranged to take place at a gym in Jesmond which was owned by Andy Webb [a former Mr Great Britain body-builder]. Andy Webb was a gentleman, Viv was a gentleman, they were all nice and friendly. I came through from Sunderland on my own. [Staggering to think that Ernie was fearless in turning up to such a venue on his own, but he did.] I never brought anyone with me. I walked in their camp on my own. There were a few of them there, and Viv got on the phone to tell Billy I was there and I was kept waiting a further hour and a half to two hours before he came.

'I remember feeling cold [owing to the lengthy wait] and Andy Webb was very good towards me and he gave me a cup of tea to warm me up because by the time Billy arrived they'd been talking for about 20 minutes around the corner. So I more or less explained to Viv that, if I sorted it out over a cup of tea without any trouble, then that's the way I preferred it. [Again, staggering to think that Ernie was as a calm as a cucumber wanting to talk things out over a cup of tea. Obviously the others there might have seen this as a sign of weakness, but Ernie is just that sort of guy. Not for one minute, though, should he have been underestimated – it wasn't for nothing that his fists were called the 'peacemakers'.]

'I didn't want any trouble, but at the same time I went through because if that was the only way to solve it, then fair enough, and Billy obviously wanted the fight on. So I went through to where they had the fight arranged. It was a small compartment, there was a little bank that went up, and obviously I realise now that was suited for Billy's needs. With me being a lot lighter, he could get me into the corner, or if I ran up the bank I would slip or fall over, which I did at one point when I was fighting, but I got out of that anyhow.

'Billy came up to me, and he was a gentleman when he approached me. The first thing he said to me was, "Ernie, I want to shake your hand now before we have this fight and I'm going to shake your hand after the fight."

'I shook his enormous hand, then we got on with the fight. Billy sort of stood in a boxer's stance. I didn't underestimate him because he's got a powerful punch and later on, as we became friends, we had a bit of trouble with someone and he has got a powerful punch. So my strategy was to wear him out and then go in for it. That was my strategy before I even went through there.

'I stood there and I jumped about a bit and I was flicking punches at him, trying to egg him on to come forward. The punches weren't really very hard; to be honest I wasn't even properly warmed up because I'd been standing waiting all that time in the cold.

'So Billy was throwing lefts, coming forward with lefts, straight lefts, and trying to catch me with them, but obviously I was jumping about a little bit, flicking a punch here and there, getting him to move, and at one stage Billy got on top of me. I managed to quickly escape from underneath his arm and I was back up on my feet in no time, because I was only 13 ½ stone at the time and I was pretty fit and agile and I could jump about a little bit.

'We stood, we bounced about a little bit again. He was trying to get his punches and I noticed he was open for a left hook. But something inside's telling me to hold that left hook back, so now I'm throwing right hands all the time and now I'm warmed up and they're coming over strong and I even said during the fight as a bit of hype, "Right, I'm warmed up now. I'm starting the fight off now."

'I don't know how long I was fighting. I cannot say if it was five minutes, but it wasn't half an hour or three-quarters of an hour, but when you think, five minutes could be a long time for most fit fellas. Anyhow, I never took any punches – I might have had to a little bit, but nothing really hard – and I came in with a right hand all the time. I've thrown a right hand and caught him with a left hook, so now I'm coming in to finish the job off.

'Billy's moving around but as he's staggering over I'm thinking, Whoa, I've been caught with an uppercut!

'But then I fell over. It was a good punch, one of my hands was on the ground, in fact, it was the left hand, and then Keith Bell come around and he got hold of my hand. I was embarrassed because I thought they were stopping the fight because I'd been knocked over. I thought Billy was now going to run in and kick me because he would have been desperate and I was going to roll around and spring back up, that was the theme that went through my mind; you're confident that that was the way it would go.

'So I knew I was vulnerable because he could have run at me and kicked me. I got up and that was the point I went berserk. I tore into him, split all his lips and that and literally went mad and shouted, "Come oooo-n!" and just literally went straight at him as if to say, I'm not getting beat off by anybody. I was really hyped up.

'Then I went forward and Viv grabbed me shouting, "Howway, Ernie! Howway, Ernie!" and things like that.

'So they stopped the fight and I was dead confused because I'd realised Billy had knocked me over, but they said, "Howway, you've beaten him fair and square."

'So then Billy went that way and Viv went the other way and I was confused, so I followed the way Viv went.

'Remember, walking away from that, I'd been involved in a fight and I'd been hit and things like that. For a minute my mind went a bit blank. As I walked through the door I remember walking into Viv and he was sitting on the seat and he was saying, "Look, I want no trouble. I want no trouble in this gym, mind."

'I said, "Look, I'll stand here with you."'

'I folded my arms and stood beside him. Andy Webb was standing there and Andy Webb's head was down like that, I didn't know why. I thought it could be because of what Viv said or he was embarrassed with the way Viv went on because he seemed to be like an honourable type of person and was nice towards me and made me feel comfortable.

'I can remember that I went to the toilet, came back and then shook Viv's hand and everything and we were all right, as I walked towards the door and went out I could feel Viv watching me from behind, I knew without turning my head. When I got out, Billy was at the other side of the door, so he must have walked around and out some other way. He come up to me and hugged me and I hugged him back and we shook hands and everything and just like what he said before the fight, that he'd shake my hand after the fight, he kept his word.

'I'd previously boxed Viv Graham and I beat him in the ring, I was too strong for him, pound for pound. I remember when I was young, I used to idolise Rocky Marciano and when I used to fight in that ring I didn't want to box and I used to think it clever to take punches, so I knew I could take a punch even though I'd boxed only a few times. At that time, I was silly. I was young and it was daft the way I went on at that time. At 17 to 18 we go through all sorts of phases when we grow up, don't we? Looking up to Rocky Marciano gave me strength. If I wanted to beat anybody, I just used to think of Rocky Marciano. He had a head like a bowling ball and you couldn't hurt him and that's the way I thought, so really a little bit of that was still in me.

'Anyway, getting back to the fight with Billy, as I was getting back into the car, Keith Bell said, "You know, Viv shouldn't have stuck that sly punch on you."

'It dawned on me what had happened and I said, "Ah, I see what you mean."

'That was when I realised that it wasn't Billy that gave me that walloping uppercut, and it all fell into place then. I got out of the car and went back into the gym and Viv was on the phone and I think Keith was in the other room, although I'm guessing about that.

'When Viv finished, he came over and said, "Ernie, look, Billy was like a dad to me, he really brought me up when I was younger."

'I said, "Look, it was only a daft punch, forget about it."

'Viv sheepishly asked, "Is it OK if I come through [to Sunderland]?"

'I said that it would be all right, but I'm always like that. Even when I got out of prison, I forgave certain people for what they'd done against me.

'But I can forgive people and I realise everybody's got good points and everybody's got bad points. I try to motivate the good points in people, which isn't a bad thing, but be careful because the bad ones will take over.

'Marciano is portrayed as a good man; his mother went to church and prayed for him. He come from an Italian type of family where his mother didn't like him getting into the ring and he didn't like his mother knowing he was getting hurt, so I suppose, in a way, when you're reading books like that as a kid, maybe it's been reflected in me and kept me off the drugs and off the streets and got me into the gym training. People wanted to be like Marciano but now people want to be like Tyson.

'After the fight with Billy, I maintained some links with Viv and we had a few discussions on the phone about it because I'd heard rumours going about that I'd been "knocked out cold for ten minutes".

'I discussed that with Viv and he explained, "Look, I haven't said anything like that, Ernie."

'He told me that he had lots of respect for me and I came through there on my own. Billy Hardy went through to Newcastle and he met with John Davison and Viv and all them and he turned around and said, "Look, all of them through there, they've got loads of respect for you."

'But I was also hearing stories. What happened once was that Gavin Cook was asking me about what went on and he said, "I've been in his [Viv's] company and he says he knocked you out for ten minutes."

'I said, "If Viv ever wants his go at me ..."

'I heard Viv was very supportive towards me over a few things because I've had trouble with the Sayers; we've chased them from Sunderland when they came with guns one night. There's a load of lads will tell you the truth about what happened there. They come barging in, it was Gary Robb who had the After Dark [nightclub], and what happened was Gary said, "Look, they've all barged in."

'Ashy [Paul Ashton, now serving a total of 31 years in prison] was there.

'I said, "Don't worry, we'll get them out."

'I went up to the two Sayers [Michael and Stephen] and said, "Look, there's all of us. Are you daft or something?"

'There were some big hefty blokes with us, so I turned around and said, "If you want trouble then we'll do it that way!"

'They turned around and said that they had guns, so I said we also had guns. "He's got one there," I said, pointing to one of the men with me. I was only bluffing but, sure enough, one of them did have one as well. He actually went to his car, came back and told me he had one, but I never saw it, but I spread that about.

'I'm not a bloke that would like to use things like that, but from my point of view it was a bit of bluff and I wanted to get them off the premises and they offered me violence and I said, "OK, then, I'll have you two together and I'm offering you two violence."

'In other words, "If that's what you want." But there's loads of scenarios happened like that around the town. Anyway, the bluff worked with them and they cleared off.

'Some time later there was talk that one of them [the Sayers] was going to come through and have a go at me. I heard that Viv went up to him and he turned around and told the lad that was with the Sayers that he was going to get knackered if he had a go at me.

'So one night when he comes through to Sunderland I sat and waited and confronted him and said, "I hear you're going to have a go at me?"

'"Nah, nah. I don't want any trouble with you," was his reply, so I just left it.

'I built up a friendship with Viv and actually went through to his house and had a cup of tea with him and had a discussion over different things.

'I remember Gavin Cook was working with Viv through there [Newcastle] and he came through and said, "I've told Viv that you're not bothered about him and I'm keeping out of it, so here's his phone number."

'He must have been match-making and I said, "I'm not going to back down from him, Gavin."

'So I pulled Viv up and quizzed, "You're the one going around telling everyone that you knocked me out for ten minutes."

'Viv countered, "Ernie, I've never said that. I've got nothing but respect for you and all I want is your respect."

'I replied, "Look, Viv, you've always had my respect. I've heard a lot about you, although the only thing that put me off was when you punched me, but you've always got my respect, but now you're going around saying you knocked me out."

'Anyway, Viv denied saying it to the end.

'I remember meeting one of Viv's friends called McNally from around where Viv had once lived in Rowlands Gill and he said, "Honestly, Ernie, Viv Graham had lots of respect for you."

'He went on to tell me that Viv was telling everyone I was "a man" and how I'd went on my own to the fight.

'There was another lad training with me in the gym and he said, "You know something, Ernie, you should never take notice of what some people say, I was training with Viv once and he's got loads of respect for you."

'I ended up getting on well with Viv, but you've always got to remember that there's still a dividing line and you do hear Chinese whispers and all that. I'd heard stories, how true they were I don't know, but he'd come and have a drink with you, he'd take you to the bar when he was ready and as you go in he'll put his arm around you and all of a sudden it's *BANG! BANG!* and he's on you.

'Other stories were that he wouldn't take his coat off and stand in front of the man, it would be something like, "You all right, mate?" and then *BANG!*, so I was advised to be wary of that sort of stroke. I kept that little bit of doubt in my mind and I was very careful of how I went about it if I ever socialised with him because he did want to come through here.

'I'd also heard that Viv liked to have an audience around him when he kicked off with a couple of lads who he might knock out and then the word spreads, "Viv knacked three lads the other night, you should've seen him."

'I mean, anybody can go and do that, but that's just the image ... but anyway it mightn't be true because you hear all kinds of stories about me, you'll hear some good and you'll hear some bad.'

Ernie's account of Viv shows what kind of man Viv was in that he broke a code of conduct for his friend and mentor, Billy Robinson, when he punched Ernie in order to give Billy some time. Billy wouldn't have approved, had he had time to say so, because afterwards he congratulated Ernie on a fair and square win.

Maybe that is not the way it was meant to go, but it did and, when Ernie felt Viv's eyes burning into his back after the fight, it might have been because Viv was overawed at Ernie's resilience to his punch. It maybe showed Viv that, if he ever had a toe-to-toe with Ernie, then, as had happened in a past boxing match between them, it would be Viv who would come off the loser.

Ernie was forgiving towards Viv and this clearly shows the kind of qualities he learned from his hero Rocky Marciano.

As for Viv spreading rumours that he had knocked Ernie out for ten minutes, it tallies with some accounts. Of course, such bravado helps maintain a hard-man image and what easier way to do it than to embroider the truth, as Viv seemed to do.

Ernie is the classic hard man. Viv was the new breed, straddling the past and present, but he didn't have the inherent safety reflex that is bred into city dwellers, and that is what was to cause his downfall.

Finally, in order to serve journalistic integrity, Stephen Sayers has been invited to add his comments about the trouble at one of Sunderland's nightspots. Here he refutes certain ideas: 'Firstly, if I was going anywhere for trouble, I would not be taking my wife and her two friends with me, who happened to be out with me that night. We arrived at the club. I knew of Ernie Bewick by reputation and asked for him at the door, out of courtesy, because I understood he was approachable, although I had never met this man before.

'While [I was] waiting in the foyer, my brother, Michael, turned up with Paul Ashton. Ashy sets eyes on the Hammer [Stephen Eastland], who also happened to be in the club at that time and they made an immediate beeline for each other. And that's how the scenario that Ernie Bewick mentions all started.

'Stevie the Hammer is a man who my brothers and me have known, personally, for a number of years and we regard him as a friend. When Ashy and the Hammer set eyes on each other, basically, it was between the two of them, knocking everybody to one side. Remember, these two men are 18 and 20 stone. This was a rick between two Geordies and nothing to do with the club or anybody else.

'Well, all hell broke loose with these two in the thick of it, then up pops Ernie Bewick, making a lot of unnecessary noise. I am a strong believer that if you're going to do something, there's no need to talk or make a show of things. The club was packed and I noticed there were four or five groups of Geordies. One stood out in particular and that was a group mainly from the West End of Newcastle. If the Devil could cast his net, he'd have had a right result that night! These men have a reputation for extreme violence, and rightly so.

'So in the middle of all this, there's Ernie Bewick storming from one end of the club to the other, shouting, "Sunderland people" this and "Sunderland people" that. As I said, I had my wife with me and the last thing I wanted was trouble.

'Mind you, all the Geordie lads were now getting the hump with this little man. At one stage, I had to plead with the West End lads not to do him, as they were all tooled to the hilt.

'I told him, "Ernie, calm yourself down because these people are tooled up and are going to do you!"

'His reply was, "We have guns as well!"

'I says, "Maybe so, but these people use them for a living, not for flash. There's one hell of a difference!"

'I came to the conclusion that this man had obviously taken too many blows to the head in his boxing career. To understand what sort of a predicament he was in, believe me when I tell you it would have resembled Custer's last stand! If he lives another 100 years, he will never come as close to getting it as he did that night.

'The West End lads would have attacked this man at once if I had not defused the situation. What thanks do I get? Well, I'll tell you … He gives himself a gee at my family's expense by saying that he not only challenged me and my brother, but he chased us from Sunderland.

'This man, the likes of him, are not capable of chasing me and my brothers in a schoolyard game of tuggy, never mind anything else. Yes, Ernie is a man who can fight and I respect him for that, but, as no doubt he will be reading this with interest, don't judge my brothers or me by the people you also associate with in Sunderland, because you have no one to compare us with. It would be right to say, "Don't get your ambitions mixed up with your capabilities."

'People in the know will tell you there are different levels of violence, fighting men and violent men. A fighting man will fight you and his object will be to knock you out and put you to sleep for a couple of minutes, whereas a violent man will put you to sleep permanently.

'If this challenge, what he describes, had taken place in my brother's presence and mine it would certainly have been accepted, but not there, and not then, and certainly not in the presence of my wife. Let me tell you, we would not have tolerated it in any shape or form. As for the Bewicks, the Cockerills and the Garsides of the North-East, all I can say is that it's fortunate for them that they are not from Tyneside, as, believe me, their antics would not be tolerated.'

Well, there you have it ... or just about. To finish on the note of John Henry Sayers, the brother of Stephen and Michael, he was released from prison after serving a long sentence for robbery. John wanted to set up a taxi company because he'd finished with crime and he knew, if he so much as released wind in the wrong direction, the police would lift him. Which was proven to be the case in the Freddie Knights murder investigation.

When Sayers submitted an application to set up and run a minicab company, his application was declined. But, rather than the rejection of John Henry Sayers's application, the issue that was on most of Newcastle's underworld lips was, how could a convicted fraudster be allowed to get away with running a security company and be paid from North One and Newcastle City Council, and how was he able to draw money from a publicly and European-funded project?

Peter Donnelly appeared before Newcastle Crown Court in a 'long firm' fraud case that involved a Welsh slate company being ripped off for £23,000; Donnelly, who had past convictions for dishonesty, burglary and resisting arrest, Section 18 assault (resulting in 18 months' imprisonment), theft, drink-driving and fraud.

Glen Gatland, defending in the fraud case, said, 'Mr Donnelly is employing over 40 people; his VAT, tax and National Insurance are being paid. In a VAT check, the VAT man came up with nothing in the company. He arranges contracts. The offence was committed 22 months ago and his business is very successful and Mr Donnelly makes an offer of full compensation to the slate company and to pay prosecution costs if given a suspended sentence.'

Mr Gatland then suggested to the judge, Judge Crawford, QC, that the sentence on Donnelly be deferred for three months.

Judge Crawford said, 'People can't buy their way out of prison.'

Councillor Tony Flynn, the then head of Newcastle City Council, was asked what he thought of such a company (DH Security) being run by a convicted felon and his reply made for interesting reading: 'The company ... would be unlikely to meet the Authority's criteria for inclusion in our standing list of contractors which the Authority would allow business to be conducted with. However, the development on which the company has been employed is a complex one, being managed by a consortium of partners in the form of a joint venture agreement with the City Council...'

5

THE KILLING OF
VIV GRAHAM

New Year's Eve 1993 was the last day of Viv's life. He was gunned down in a side road off High Street West in Wallsend as he walked towards his powerful Ford Sierra Cosworth. The 'Cossie' had become his pride and joy when he replaced his BMW with it. It was self-bestowed and the only real luxury he allowed himself that reflected his near-celebrity status. The boy from the village of Highfield had almost made it and here was his proof. The metallic burgundy Cosworth reflected the sodium streetlights from its gleaming paintwork. A lone toy monkey dangled from the rear-view mirror like a lucky mascot warding off evil.

The cigarettes and dog food he was carrying in his mighty hands signified the things Viv loved in life – the cigarettes were for his fiancée, whom he worshipped, and the dog food represented his love of animals. Here he was on New Year's Eve, thinking of the ones he loved and on his way back home to them.

As Viv left the shop he wished the shopkeeper 'Happy New Year' and they shook hands. There would not be any late-night revelling for him because his fiancée, Anna Connelly, was not feeling too well. Anna stayed home, knowing her beloved Viv would soon be resting in his favourite position, with his feet up on the couch among those closest to him and with the phone off the hook.

But, in Viv's head, troubled thoughts must have been threatening this image of serene and contented domesticity. While he had been in a pub, passing time with friends and acquaintances, he had received a death threat.

'It's for you, Viv,' the manager of the New Anchor pub had said as he passed Viv the phone.

'I've just had a death threat,' Viv had remarked moments later, his voice apparently quite normal.

Viv always kept his innermost fears hidden from those looking for a chink in his armour – it didn't do to show this lot his real self. But a part of his fear shone through like a shaft of sunlight passing through a dark cloud on a wet, but sunny day. A few of those present had caught a glimpse of what they thought was a slight change in Viv's composure, but it wasn't wise to let him know they had seen this.

For Viv was the man that no one messed with, there was no one capable of doing him in, and anyway he was always getting death threats from some peeved character. Some upstart waging war over the phone because they knew they could not do anything physically to him in a one-to-one. What did Viv have to fear? These threats, after all, were ten a penny and it was probably just another wind-up, as all the previous ones had been. As far as he was concerned, it sucked, like all the rest.

Besides, Viv had more important things on his mind. He had just telephoned his secret lover, Gillian Lowes, and told her he would be ringing at midnight to wish her a happy New Year. There was not a day that went by when he did not have her or their two children on his mind. It was a busy time of year and he would be in demand as usual, as there was always some plonker ready to cause trouble at the drop of a hat.

Viv was on call 24 hours a day, 365 days of the year. If anyone on Tyneside could not get Viv on the phone, they may as well have called the Samaritans for help because no one else would be of any use. When people made a 999 emergency call, they may as well have heard, 'Emergency, which service do you require police, fire, ambulance or Viv?'

Viv knew this and was starting to get weary of his profession as a troubleshooter. After all, he had been in this line of business for nearly 17 years. Complacency had crept in. Whereas at one time he would be extra security conscious, now he had become too relaxed and lethargic over his safety. He had forgotten the lesson that he was taught in 1989 when he was shot at outside Manhattan's. This should have kept him on his toes, although some five years had gone by and time had healed his memories of that extremely close call. His vision of being executed gangland style was of a leather-clad motorcyclist riding alongside his car and shooting him through the window.

Viv had credited his potential killers with too much intelligence. He used his fists; he was not a man for guns or other weapons. The only time he used a gun was when he went hunting game with his father. He had conjured up the motorcyclist-hitman scenario from movies he used to watch. In reality, it would be a rare motorcyclist that could pull that one over on Viv – because he was ready. He had his own idea of how his life would end and his premonition was half-right. Yes, his car was involved and, yes, a window. Maybe, in his death fantasy, Viv saw the motorcyclist's helmet as a means of disguise for his killer.

This ability to home in on what could happen should have served as a warning. Maybe Viv had become accustomed to overriding his sixth sense over the years. But alarm bells should have started ringing when that threatening phone call was received, no matter how often he received them. The dread of something happening must have given him a brief shock, but because he had faced such threats before, his adrenalin just did not pump like it used to at the beginning of his career.

Viv could camouflage his feelings like a Red Indian covering his trail and, anyway, the call was soon masked by all the other thoughts of what he had to do, becoming a haze in his mind. Too much was going on in his head: what was happening that night, as well as tomorrow, when he would be seeing his parents and Gillian and his kids. Not forgetting to collect the cigarettes and dog food at the corner shop on the way back to his car seemed more important than thinking of when a strike against his life might happen.

This was a time of year to relax, de-stress and hang out with friends and that's what Viv was doing. He was in the Anchor pub from 4.15pm, and from there he walked just a few yards to the Queen's Head, before leaving at 6.05pm and calling into a corner shop on his way to his car.

The Anchor, the Queen's Head and the shop were all on the same side of the road, so he did not have to cross back and forth over Wallsend High Street. Anybody watching for him coming out of either pub could have done so easily from across the road. The only road he had to cross was Border Road, which adjoined the High Street. People were making their way to a nearby bingo.

Nah! Viv must have thought. No one's going to be daft enough to do anything here. He would soon be cocooned in the womb-like safety of his beloved Cosworth and be back at home in a flash, back to loving Anna; she would soothe away his stressed-out headache.

Within five seconds of leaving the corner shop, Viv was at the side of his Cossie. It was dark, even though it was only just after 6.05pm. His keys were in his hand; he was looking at the key fob, holding the items he had bought in the shop and thinking that he would be home soon. He was now in sight of his killers.

Most people have done it: been carrying some items, fumbled with a set of keys in the dark and not been sharp enough to notice somebody walk past. Maybe the other person said 'Hello' or something. To a degree, they have lost concentration and co-ordination and for a split second are oblivious to what is going on around them.

As Viv neared his car, something looked different, but he could not quite decide what it was. His mind was not thinking as straight as it normally did: he had lots to think about as it was the festive season, and his system had been slowed down by the odd seasonal drink, for Viv was not used to drinking anything more than a few halves of Guinness. Was the window on the car door broken? Was that it?

Just then, a man called out something to him from a car coming out of a back lane on to Border Road. Viv automatically turned around to look, just as when someone calls out your name or whistles loudly you cannot help but look; it is a conditioned reflex.

The killer knew what to shout to get Viv's attention. *BLAM!* The gunshot echoed off the wall of the dark back lane. The first bullet fired at Viv from the .357 Magnum was from a range of only five yards or so. From a handgun powerful enough to penetrate metal armour and kill large game! In the USA, the .357 Magnum's use as a police weapon began to be curtailed in the 1960s. It had proven very effective against criminals – too effective, according to the protests it sparked off!

All that Viv would have seen would have been the flash from the barrel, followed by fiery pain milliseconds later. The shot ringing out in the normally quiet street had telegraphed to those within hearing range that something menacing was going on.

Viv's first reactions, according to police forensic reports, were still pretty swift now that he knew he was under attack and that this was really happening. Before the first bullet had completed its journey through his thigh, entering from the outside, his hand shot down so fast between his thighs that it is thought that as the bullet left that leg it nicked the edge of his hand, which was there ahead of the bullet! The bullet then continued its blood-splattering route into his other thigh and exited the other side, causing a searing pain.

Now that Viv's legs were disabled, he hit the ground like a broken statue. Although the underworld claimed later that the hit was only meant as a warning to Viv, the gunman was too far gone in the head.

BLAM! The second shot was the killer shot, which ripped apart Viv's lower abdomen before the bullet passed out of his side, leaving damaged organs in his muscled torso. Haemorrhaging was so bad that nothing in the long term would have saved Viv. A melon-sized hole was visible in his side. A third shot fired at Viv when he was down had not made full contact with him. Police forensic evidence suggested that the bullet may have struck the ground and ricocheted off the solid surface and zipped over Viv's body as he lay there, leaving a line on his back.

Viv would not have understood what had really happened to him. He must have felt abandoned and lonely as he started to obey his survival instinct to find safety. To any normal man, that would have been it! But Viv summoned up what was left of his enormous strength and started to crawl back towards the High Street.

The shopkeeper ran out to see what had gone on, even though it would have been a more natural thing to shy away from such a sinister sound. By now, Viv was pulling his bullet-ridden body with his tree-like arms, past the shop towards the pub. To the shopkeeper, who wished to remain anonymous, it was obvious that the bullets had passed straight through him, leaving gaping wounds.

Twenty-five yards away was the Queen's Head pub. Blind instinct must have been the only thing leading Viv back the way he had came, only this time it was a crawling, bleeding, dying Viv that was seen through the window of the pub by Terry Scott, a friend and associate.

Without any concern for his own safety, Terry ran out to Viv. Unbeknownst to him, the two killers had already left the area, speeding off in a stolen blue Ford Escort.

As Viv lay there bleeding on the pavement he had the sense of decorum to pull his shirt down over his main wound, as if signifying one last act of neatness. Then, as he lay there dying, he asked his friend to lift him to his feet.

'I can't let them see me like this,' he said.

One last fight.

'I'm going. I'm going.'

Terry leaned protectively over Viv; he could see there was a lot of damage to Viv's body. To make it worse, there was nothing he could do to help; his own large, powerful body was useless, and the white shirt he wore seemed to draw attention to the tragic scene as others gathered around.

Watching the life drain out of someone you had minutes earlier been wishing a 'Happy New Year' was a daunting sight for Terry. No matter how hard or how big you are, your heart is just about the same as the next man's. Nothing in life prepares you for this sort of thing. No movie or TV drama could ever capture such a feeling of impending loss.

For a while, Terry cradled Viv's head. What an emotional sight that must have been. 'Big boys don't cry.'

He was caught up in a gangland shooting. Viv could have asked him to accompany him home from the pub if he had felt uncomfortable at the threat made over the phone. But he didn't. That is how little effect it had had on Viv. Yet it's difficult not to reflect on the pressure put on him by the almost daily ritual of death threats that marked the last years of his short life.

Awake! for morning in the Bowl of Night
Has flung the Stone that puts the Stars to Flight:
And Lo! the Hunter of the East has caught
The Sultan's Turret in a noose of Light

Dreaming when Dawn's Left Hand was in the Sky,
I heard a voice within the Tavern cry,

'Awake, my little ones, and fill the cup
Before Life's Liquor in its Cup be dry.'
And as the Cock crew, those who stood before
The Tavern shouted – 'Open then the Door!
You know how little while we have to stay,
And once departed, may return no more.'

Now the New Year reviving old Desires,
The thoughtful Soul to solitude retires.

The Rubaiyat of Omar Khayyam

Profile of Terry Scott

March 1995: Scott is shot at six times in Newcastle in
what was possibly a revenge attack for his cradling
Viv's head. He sustains no injuries and jumps over a
fence to safety. The police do not connect the attack to
Viv's murder some 15 months earlier. No one is
apprehended for the shooting, but spent cartridges are
found near the scene. The gunman is identified as
wearing a crash helmet and this description fits with
that of a similar gunman-style accessory used in later
Tyneside shootings.

December 1995: Scott, 35, starts to show signs that
the pressures from his past traumas are getting to him.
Witnessing a friend lying close to death in his arms and,
in a later incident, being shot at himself, cannot have
made life easy for him.

While employed as a doorman at Newcastle's Bliss
nightspot Scott allegedly assaults a male clubber in a
queue-jumping argument. The victim suffers a fractured
depressed cheekbone and surgery is needed to rebuild

that part of his face. Scott has not had the support that a professional person would have had if they had been through the same sort of trauma. A professional would have had the help of a team to handle such stress. Where could Scott offload his stress?

He continues working, as he is entitled to do under the Club Doorman Registration Scheme, because, although he is on bail awaiting trial, he is pleading 'not guilty', and remains innocent until proven guilty. A professional in comparison could be suspended on full pay, whatever the reason for the suspension, until proven guilty.

February 1997: The jury in the assault case fails to reach a verdict. Scott continues to work as a doorman, as he is entitled to.

October 1997: Scott is back in the dock. This time he pleads guilty, clearly having received legal advice that he could face a custodial sentence if found guilty. The advice to 'Take the wrap and walk' leads to a 12-month prison sentence, suspended for two years.

Scott has to leave his job at Ram Jam's bar in Newcastle's Bigg Market when his licence is withdrawn because of the criminal conviction recorded against him, as the rules of Club Doorman Registration Scheme demand. He becomes, allegedly, a taxi driver.

The festive merriment of the night was shattered, and for those devoted to Viv and around at that time, the echoes of the three gunshots would reverberate in their memories for years to come.

As Viv lay in the ambulance, his body was going into involuntary shock. A lone police officer sat in the ambulance as it sped off to hospital, and witnessed the ambulance crew restart Viv's heart when it stopped. Against all the odds, and miraculously, the crew managed to get his heart going again. What would have killed an ordinary mortal immediately had not quite done that. This was Viv Graham, no ordinary man. What must have been going through his mind at that time?

Anna Connelly had been informed almost straight away and she made her way to North Tyneside General Hospital as fast as she could, arriving ahead of the ambulance. The hospital was starting to fill up with a lot of anxious people awaiting news of Viv's condition. His powerfully built father, Jack, gazed into nothingness with his deep-brown eyes that were so good at camouflaging pain, just like Viv's. Jack willed his son to live and would have traded places with him at once if it could have saved him from death.

Peter Connelly, Anna's brother, arrived at the hospital and the scene that greeted him must have looked like bedlam. He was moved by the amount of people he saw. Terry Scott was running around venting his frustration on the walls with punches that would have floored Mike Tyson.

On seeing her fiancé, Anna was told by him: 'I love you.'

The doctor knew there was no hope; even if Viv had managed to stay alive, he could not have survived the huge hole in his side. Jack told Anna that his son would pull through, but she knew that the severity of Viv's wounds meant the end of his life.

In the final throes of death, Viv suffered a massive heart attack. How could the doctor tell the highly agitated group of relations, friends and associates who packed the hospital waiting area that the man they all willed to live was dead?

Viv's body was placed in the recovery room, where, in death, he looked quite normal. Later that evening, when things had calmed down, Viv was pronounced dead at 10.20 after being formally identified by his father.

This was now a murder inquiry headed by Detective Chief Superintendent Barry Stewart, head of Northumbria Police's CID.

By now, Viv's supposed friends had gone into hiding, fearing that they were next on the hit list. Pubs and clubs on Tyneside closed that night for fear of reprisal attacks. Word of Viv's death travelled via the taxi drivers of Newcastle.

The blue Ford Escort used by the killers had been in the area for a while. It was parked in a shadowy back lane near where Viv usually parked; he was becoming a man of habit and this made it easier for the murderers to strike with certainty. They sat impatiently waiting for Viv to appear around the corner. The police could not determine if the shots were fired from the passenger or the driver's side of the Escort. Viv had parked near a litter-bin area in Border Road, which gave the killers a better chance of carrying out the job successfully as he was hemmed in and so an easier target.

There is a question mark over whether the window of Viv's car was already broken so as to distract his attention from the killers or a bullet fired at him smashed it. An investigation has determined that there is a strong likelihood that the window was broken before he returned to the car. Viv had been warned in the past to watch out if he came back to his car and found the window was broken or the car had a flat tyre, as it could be a stalling tactic in a killing set-up.

A man was seen leaving the Queen's Head only minutes before Viv left. The then second in command of the case was Detective Chief Inspector Keith Felton, who described the man they sought in connection with this line of enquiry as being five feet two in height, with short, cropped, mousy hair. The man walked east, along the High Street, in the same direction as Viv when he left the pub. Was this man signalling to the killers who lay in wait that Viv was on his way?

After the killers had struck, they drove off fast in the stolen Escort with the lights out. The police suggested that they may have travelled west, along Shields Road, turned right into Benfield Road, then left into Rothbury Terrace before finally dumping the car in Simonside Terrace, Heaton, where it was set on fire.

A later report stated that a woman had nearly been knocked over by a Blue Ford Escort in Debdon Gardens, only a minute's drive from Simonside Terrace. This part is important and the reader should remember it in preparation for something that is looked into later in this book.

Detective Superintendent John May, who has since retired, had now taken over charge of the murder investigation. A blonde woman was seen in a street near where Viv was murdered at the time of the shooting and police sought her. She was spotted in a doorway of a corner shop on the junction of Border Road and the High Street. A very good description of her was given: she was in her early twenties, had blonde, collar-length, curly hair and was wearing blue jeans and a dark, hipster-type jacket.

There were two independent witnesses to the incident and their statements put the blonde woman on the other side of the High Street. After Viv was shot, she was put as being near his body as she went across the road towards the shop.

The getaway car had been stolen earlier in the day from Durham Road, Birtley, near Chester-le-Street, between 2.30pm and 3.30pm, which seems to have been leaving it a bit late for using it as a getaway car in a drive-by shooting.

Although the murder had been planned for some time, the killers had dragged their feet over carrying it out and, for some reason, were now apparently acting hastily over finalising the matter. Was it that the instigators were becoming impatient at the time this was taking?

The logical approach would have been to steal the car some days beforehand rather than on the very day of the murder. That way it would have been checked and ready for use and not so fresh in the memories of police officers who would have been looking for the blue Escort, which had been reported stolen the same day it was used in the murder.

It was also discovered that telephone calls to Viv's home asking where he was were similar to calls made to the two pubs Viv had visited that day. The killers may have been keeping tabs on his whereabouts, in preparation for striking at their target. In any event, they located Viv in one of the pubs he was in that day.

Witnesses saw the Escort drive by and the killers fire three shots. For them to see the car drive by it had to have come out of the back lane into Border Road, where Viv's car was parked, and this meant that information indicating that the killer had shot from the driver's window was correct. The car would have driven into Border Road, away from the direction of the High Street. The murder looked like it had been stage-managed by others who had the killers acting like puppets for them. It appeared that the plot had been designed by someone reasonably intelligent, but the killing did not fall into the classic type of drive-by shooting, in which the car passes within feet of the victim, almost side on.

6

THE HITMAN'S TRIAL

When someone wants to have another person bumped off or hurt, it is almost invariably done by one or more individuals among his or her associates or extended family. Very rarely is the killer unknown to the victim. A hitman gives his opinion on whether Viv Graham's killers were professionals: 'The boys from Newcastle were fucking each other up faster than you could say "snuff videos". They have a name for being head cases, not because they could frighten anyone but because they was always shooting, stabbing or slashing each other up.

'Whenever I was doing any killings, I would always make sure that I had no drugs in me. If there was a chance of being caught, I needed to keep my wits about me and know what I was saying. I used to keep a solicitor on a retainer, a man called Barrington Black from Leeds. He was the best there was at his job; that was way back, he's retired now, maybe even dead. I didn't really need his services but it would have paid off if I needed bail; he could get a three-legged donkey bail if need be. When the Newcastle lads did a job they worried about that sort of thing later on and usually would end up with some geezer wearing a wig telling them to plead guilty and they'd get them off with a seven or ten stretch.

'My job is an art form, carried out by a craftsman. I know some of the lads from up there [Newcastle] and when I've met them they struck me as careless in what they were up to. They'd have to brag about things that made them look the part. The careless part was when they'd brag about things that they said they'd done to people who owed them money or when they gave someone a sorting out for some other reason.

'They didn't know me by my real name and I only accompanied my business pals to meetings when I was asked to attend in case of trouble, as a lot of taxing was going on around the country. These were semi-legit deals that would involve large sums of cash, as certain deals could only be paid for in cash. These weren't drug deals; they were deals for hooky spirits that duty hadn't been paid on. The booze was meant to go abroad but had come straight out of the Bonded Warehouses through the back door.

'My job was to make sure that no one ripped them off or taxed them for the money, which at times was over a couple of big ones [£200,000]. Any signs of trouble, then it was down to me to have taken precautions and a lot of those precautions the Geordies didn't know about and still wouldn't have if anything funny had gone on.

'There's more ways than one to skin a cat. Any cat trying to take the cash wouldn't have lasted long, they'd have been allowed to take the cash and then the fun would have begun. Within a minute of taking the cash, they would have been blown to kingdom come because the case carrying the money always had a wad of money that was hollow, and that's where I came into it.

'There are some people as bright as a dud spark plug in how they did things and I couldn't believe how they could get away with the things that they said they'd done. [Author's note: Before the interview, this man told me of criminal acts that he alleged others had carried out. At no time did he state to me that he had committed any crime himself.]

'There were only a handful of people in Newcastle that had any pull [respect] down here and one of them was Viv Graham. I'd heard how he was a bit of a handful and could handle himself. Millsie [Howard Mills] was from this way and word got back that he'd been [knee]capped. Nothing was put to me about it; I don't put the feelers out for work, I don't work that way. It wasn't unusual for me to be called in if there'd been a bit of aggro that needed sorting and I used to keep my fingers on the web in case I got the call and I'd be prepared with the background information.

'I'd travel between Glasgow and London. Anything that went down in between these two places, I used to pick up on from contacts that I had in the main cities. It wasn't a case of someone just turning up with some money and saying go and do something! That wasn't usual and if it were like that then they'd get ignored. I had to do groundwork and from all the groundwork that I did I had a full dossier on my target. I've seen me build up a picture of someone and then wait for a call to say I should do whatever it was and nothing ever happened.

'In respect of how Viv was done, you don't go with

someone else on this sort of job, as they are a liability and could drop you in it if caught and if what you say [is right] about there being two, one driver and one shooter, then that's a dead giveaway for a start.

'You don't hurt innocent people and this was in a built-up area, you say, with people in and out of boozers with a chippy nearby. It doesn't stand to reason as to why they'd need all those witnesses and risk hurting someone else nearby. The law doesn't like it when the public gets hurt. Do your own sort in, but don't hurt the public because, if you do that, you get them coming down on you so fucking hard you end up getting hurt.

'The stolen car bit's fine, but it would have really had to have been stolen some time before and not on the day because the law would have it in their heads and you'd risk getting nicked in it before the job was done or on the way to the job with the shooter on. I mean, they didn't even give it a set of moody plates; they were amateurs and hadn't killed before, that is certain! You'd be driving around in a freshly nicked car with a gun powerful enough to stop an elephant. No thanks. Just for that you'd get enough time in nick to make the clothes you were wearing just coming back into fashion the second time around by the time you got out.

'The best vehicle to use would have been a van with a side-loading door and there's a way you don't even need to have the door open to use a gun. You don't tell anybody what you're going to do, and if you recall when I told you about the Geordies having to brag about what they did, then it fingers [points to] the job being in-house.

'They had to call your man on the phone saying they were going to kill him. Talk about as thick as pig's shit. I'll tell you now, just about for certain, that this was no professional hit. They want locked up and the key thrown away for being so daft. How they got away with it, I just don't know. If there were two involved in the car, then there would have been others involved as well.

'If a car was used in a hit, then it always had to be fired, but there are better ways than that. You've got a crowded area on a New Year's Eve, that is a real bad time to do a hit because people remember the date, witnesses can recall things much more clearly when they've a particular date to recall, such as November the 5th or April Fool's Day. It wasn't clever giving the witnesses a date to remember. Even in 20 years' time, that date would stick in a witness's head.

'Another thing was to find out the person's birthday so as that would be avoided as a killing date, as any family would remember that date if they became a witness! Viv would have known the killers or people responsible for organising the killing. Pinpointing someone for doing the job ... well, it's usually always those who are close to the person in some way, such as a friend or a fellow businessman or ex-partner, a friend who has become an enemy or something related to women.

'Using the type of shooter they did, it was likely they would be drawing a lot of attention to themselves with the clout it had. A body shot isn't guaranteed to kill, even with bullets as big as the ones used. Something better than that is called a "double tap" – it's a shot to the head and one in the heart, to guarantee the job's done properly. The SAS are famous for this type of hit, but it was used by the underworld long before the SAS adopted it. The back of the head is the target because the likelihood of recovering from that alone is doubtful. All the main wires run down from that part.

'The other thing is that someone like Viv wouldn't have had a hit carried out on him by anyone from my standing. Viv would have been warned about a possible hit, but he wouldn't have been told who had asked for it to be done. The job wouldn't have been taken on; obviously it would have had to go to a grafter out to make a name for themselves. They like to do that, do a job to get a name, but it doesn't work like that because as soon as that's happened they get used, time and time again, for other dirty business because it turns into blackmail. I've seen it happen and it's not funny seeing someone forced to do something against his or her will. They've lost it then and are too dangerous to be around, they'd spill the beans on their old doll if it meant saving their own skin.

'As for a woman being involved in Viv's killing, women don't think like men. Men think like snakes, and that's been scientifically proven. Men can look at women differently to how a woman would think he was looking at her. How do I know this? Because everything's taken into account. Mind you, women are useful when having involvement in criminal actions because they can act as a distraction in more ways than one.

'We've got Viv crawling along the ground with more blood coming out of him than is in a blood bank and this shopkeeper takes his eyes off Viv and notices a blonde woman. Doesn't that show you how a man thinks? A blonde woman distracts him.

'She changed the whole thing and distracted people away from what was going on. The blonde could have been there to keep Viv's attention on her so he didn't notice the killer; she could have called out his name or indicated to the killer that Viv was on his way. There's nothing wrong with a woman standing about, maybe fumbling in her bag for something, it's normal. There's any amount of possibilities, but women aren't as cold-blooded as men, so for her to be involved there'd have to be a strong reason, especially as she walked over the road to look at him crawling the opposite way she was headed.

'People tend to think that a woman won't be noticed and can blend in – not women with blonde hair, though? The things a woman does make her appear normal, but a blonde always gets attention. She could have been checking the state of his injuries so as to let the killer know how good his shot was. Viv wouldn't have been the hardest person to find and all of these people involved shows the poor way it's been carried out.

'I just can't think how no one's had their collar felt for it and been put away. They'll think they can do anything now and that'll be their downfall. One of them will do something way over the top and get collared for it and you can bet they'll drop the killer right in the shit. That's why I'm a loner. I'm not going to grass myself up.'

Uncannily, what this hitman said back in 1998 has some relevance to another case. Two men murdered Paul Logan, 25, a pizza delivery driver from Shotley Bridge, Northumberland, two nights before Christmas 1993, seven days before Viv was killed. It is claimed that the same two men responsible for this murder could also be responsible for killing Viv, although new evidence suggests otherwise.

Joe Marshall, a convicted gunman, gave evidence to the police naming the alleged killers of Paul Logan. Further claims are that £5,000 was paid to the two men to beat him up but they went too far and accidentally killed him.

The Geordie Mafia fraternity has it that one of the two

killers is definitely a heavyweight informant who gets away with selling drugs under the watchful eye of the police, while it is claimed that the second man is said to have served a term in prison for offences of violence. To date, neither man has been charged in connection with Logan's murder.

In a twist to the tale, one police officer received a three-month prison sentence for misconduct as a public official following an arson attack on a van belonging to Hugh Logan, Paul's father. The man responsible for the petrol-bomb attack, Keith Suddick, 36, was jailed for carrying out the attack, in Shotley Bridge.

High-ranking criminals are seemingly falling over themselves to be as helpful as they can to the police over Viv's murder – but only in order to receive more lenient prison sentences when caught for serious crimes!

David Glover Jr gave a statement to the police about Viv's murder, but it was pure invention, designed to help him get off with his dastardly crime of kidnapping and torturing small-time criminal Billy Collier. Glover had high hopes of going as a supergrass against the Sayers brothers Stephen and Michael. By blaming them for Viv's murder, he anticipated that he would walk free from court for his own vicious crime. He ended up being found guilty of the kidnap and torture charges and was sentenced to ten years in prison.

Glover's hopes of an acquittal had been dashed and after his conviction he became stubborn over his invented murder statement. At Glover's torture trial, Detective Chief Inspector Keith Felton put in a statement (known as a 'text') to the court confirming that he had been working as an informant for Northumbria Police since September 1992 under the pseudonym of 'Adrian

Scott'. Glover's job was to gather information about Newcastle's Conroy family and others.

Later, it was alleged that Glover had said things in relation to Viv's murder but that he was not right in the head and could not be believed. After Glover was imprisoned, he made a bid for further help in having his sentence cut. Here is a précis of what Glover told two visiting police officers, DC J Bower and DC A Trotter, at HM Prison Birmingham, on Wednesday, 22 February 1995 at 1.30pm: 'Glover was shown by DCs Trotter and Bower a video recording of Sackville Road, Newcastle upon Tyne. Glover indicated an area of bungalows in the street stating that the murderers of Viv Graham had gone to one of them after the killing. When asked how he knew this Glover said, "I drove the getaway car."

'When asked what exactly he meant Glover said, "I drove the getaway car after the shooting." When asked who did the shooting he said, "Michael Sayers."

'Glover was asked to tell the story of his involvement from the beginning and gave the following story:

'He stole an old, blue Escort from Birtley from a car park near the baths. He took it by jiggling the locks. He was with Michael Sayers at the time and they drove to Heaton, in Newcastle, parking the car somewhere in Sackville Road.

'They arranged that Glover should collect Michael Sayers later that day. In the middle of the afternoon, Glover collected Sayers in the stolen car and was directed to various places looking for Viv Graham. Sayers said he was going to shoot Graham in the legs in retaliation for some ongoing dispute. They went to Graham's house but his car was not there. They then drove around Wallsend and discovered Graham's car parked in a street off the High Street next to a flowerbed.

'Glover parked the stolen car in a back lane with a view of the back of Graham's car and Sayers walked over to Graham's car and smashed the driver's window. Glover stated that he saw the hazard warning lights flashing and assumed the alarm had been set off. He could see that Sayers was walking up and down the street where the car was parked. Then he heard three shots fired, looked and saw Graham on all fours beside the car. Sayers ran back to the stolen Escort, got in and Glover drove off.

'Glover stated he was directed which way to drive, eventually arriving at a back lane somewhere in Heaton. He torched the car and both he and Michael Sayers were picked up by Stephen Sayers and Tony Leach in a burgundy Shogun vehicle.

'Glover stated that Sayers had used a .357 Magnum, which was grey in colour, which he kept in a shoulder holster and always carried. He stated he believed Sayers was high on cocaine at the time and that they both believed Graham was only wounded.

'It was pointed out to Glover that all of the details of the murder had been well publicised and that he had not told us anything about the way the shooting was carried out that could not have been read in a newspaper. He was asked if he could give any details which would add credence to his story. He said that during the getaway drive he hit something, damaging the front of the car and that he believed the car was a woman's because it had a box of tissues and some furry toys in it.

'He also said that he had a tape recording of Michael Sayers bragging about the shooting. This had been recorded without Sayers's knowledge at a Karaoke night in a Newcastle pub. Glover claimed to have the tape in safekeeping, but would not disclose where. He also said that there were other things he could say that would convince us his story was true, but that he'd save these until a later time.

'At the time Glover gave this account he was in a restraining body belt having previously self-inflicted injuries on his wrists and damaged his cell. We pointed out to Glover that in the circumstances any further conversation held on the subject would be with his legal representative. He stated he would be happy to repeat his account and give further details of the incident in an interview in the presence of his solicitor, Mr Harrison. He was informed that we would arrange to interview him at the earliest convenient opportunity with his legal representative. At 2.20pm that day the visit with Glover was concluded.'

The murders of Paul Logan and Viv Graham, according to anonymous police claims, are similar in that the same MO was used. Both victims were lured away from where they were just before the murders by a telephone call. It is probable that both victims knew their assailants. Each murder was for revenge and, because of this, Northumbria Police are aware that the same assailants could have killed both men some few days apart. The assailants' propensity for violence is well known to Northumbria Police.

The murder of small-time Newcastle cocaine dealer Freddie Knights, 38, on 20 September 2000, is particularly relevant here as it reveals how low those higher echelons of the crime world will stoop when breaking the biggest taboo there is to break within their circle – becoming a supergrass. Within the underworld this is an act of betrayal that cannot be forgotten, far less forgiven, and is classed as being in the same rank as paedophilia. So when someone becomes a supergrass it's an absolute certainty that they have not done so out of the goodness of their heart.

Supergrass and self-confessed underworld killer and drug dealer Lee Shaun Watson, 35, from Gateshead, headed the gangland-style hit on Freddie Knights. Scar-faced Watson had hoped to get away with the hit when he heaped the blame on the unsuspecting John Henry Sayers (also known as John Henry and JHS).

John Henry had been released from prison only a short while after serving 11 years of a 15-year sentence for what has been claimed was his masterminding of and participation in a daring £350,000 robbery. After leaving prison, he had made a concerted effort to go straight, but his application to set up a taxi business was blocked by Northumbria Police, who objected to his holding the operator's licence needed to run such a business.

John Henry is considered to be one of the most poised and unruffled underworld figures ever to come out of Newcastle. For him, such a setback was not a defeat but merely a temporary brake on his ambition to go straight. Being clean-cut and clean living was part of his ethos; he abhorred the use of drugs and did not even drink alcohol.

Northumbria Police still considered John Henry to be their number-one target and, in an unremitting way, set about maintaining surveillance and updating intelligence reports on him. Unruffled by this renewed vigour in targeting him, John Henry continued to seek out ways to make an honest living.

When Freddie Knights was cruelly killed on his mother's doorstep in a shotgun attack, it was to lead to a £20-million murder inquiry that was to see psychopathic Lee Shaun Watson, the self-professed joint second in command of a criminal outfit he called the Firm, turn supergrass after he was quizzed by police over the killing of Mr Knights while in prison for possessing heroin worth £25,000 with intent to supply.

It was on 13 October 2000, only weeks after Knights was murdered, that Watson was a passenger in a car driven by Dale Miller when it went through a red traffic light. A passing police car gave chase. Miller and Watson ran off, and when Watson was cornered by the police he had to be hit with a truncheon to disarm him after he threatened officers with a lock knife. After being found in possession of the £25,000 stash of heroin, he was given three years in prison. Some would say it was a pretty light sentence.

During his time in prison, Watson was visited regularly by his girlfriend, Vanya Alan, who lived in Highfield, Gateshead. During one of these prison visits, the police covertly recorded what was said between them via a hidden microphone. Watson subsequently pleaded guilty to the murder of Knights and the invention of his outlandish story that John Henry was the boss of the Firm and that three others, Michael Dixon, 34, Eddie Stewart, 39, and Dale Miller, 38, were runners working under him.

At the Freddie Knights murder trial, during cross-examination by Jonathan Goldberg QC, Watson was asked if the heroin he had been caught with was payment for the hit on Knights.

'No,' Watson answered.

Mr Goldberg went on, 'You asked Dale Miller if he would take the rap for these £25,000 worth of drugs?'

'No.'

'You asked Miller to say it was his heroin?'

'No.'

'Do you know a man named Mickey Conroy?'

'Yes.'

'Has he anything to do with drugs?'

'I think so.'

During further cross-examination, Watson told of how he took Vanya Alan with him to a field where he test-fired a shotgun he had bought for £120 and that she also test-fired it.

Mr Goldberg asked Watson about an incident on 4 September 2000, only 16 days before the killing of Knights, in which Watson attacked a property at Hardman Gardens, Ryton, Gateshead.

Mr Duff for the prosecution: 'Kathleen Median, the occupant, had a partner who was a supposed drug dealer. When the house was vacated at 12.15pm, Watson ransacked the house, firing shots from a 4.10 sawn-off shotgun into the headboard of the bed (twice) and shooting out a window and a mirror as well as ripping sinks out. Within half an hour the police called to a house that Watson was in; he was seen to pedal away on a bicycle. Watson evaded capture until 15 September. Further evidence that Watson had been in the property was found in fingerprint evidence.'

Watson admitted to being a career criminal and that his earnings from drug dealing, racketeering and pimping netted him £175,000 per year. He admitted that Knights's little empire would have earned the firm £100,000 a year when Knights was ousted from the estate he supplied.

Mr Goldberg said to Watson, 'I suggest you're a ruthless man and are prepared to shoot someone if you can get away with it?'

Watson lied when he replied, 'No.'

In fact, he had shot someone in the head with a live .22

bullet during some after-hours drinking in a pub. The drug-crazed victim had done little more than antagonise Watson. When Watson pulled the trigger, the victim was bobbing his head about and so ended up with superficial damage.

'Once Freddie was shot in the leg I would take over the drug dealing on the estate,' Watson testified.

He was asked: 'Mickey Conroy, you knew he dealt in drugs ... Did he ever suggest taking over Freddie Knights's estate as far as drug dealing was concerned?'

Whereas previously he said he knew Conroy, this time he said, 'I don't know Mickey Conroy.'

Watson was digging himself into a deep hole. On 8 March 2002, he entered a guilty plea to the charge of murdering Knights. His remaining co-defendants had all entered 'not guilty' pleas. So it must have been a daunting prospect for Watson when he considered playing this game of the badly done by hitman.

In court and during his session in the witness box, Watson was allowed break after break after break and in all he could not have spent more than 12 hours in the dock over a four-day period. When Vanya Alan gave evidence, she admitted that the police had given her a sum in the region of £25,000 in witness-protection payments to assist her and her mother.

Heroin junkie and gang member Stephen Carlton escaped the wrath of the law when he received a healthy payout of £23,000 from Northumbria Police and escaped robbery charges when he gave evidence against those he should have been standing next to. Carlton allegedly housed some of the gang members after the killing. Yet he walked free.

Watson's plea for clemency from the witness box was: 'I'm giving evidence because I agreed to shoot Freddie

Knights in the legs, not murder him. I would not have agreed to have him shot in the head, so why should I take the blame?'

'Mickey Conroy got Lee Watson to murder Viv Graham after Viv had beaten him up in a fight on Newcastle's Quayside,' said John Henry Sayers from the witness box. It was a very bold statement that took everyone aback, but it is thought to have been nothing more than a retaliatory remark aimed at a particular man who had stood in a court dock in the mid-1990s and had sworn away the lives of the Sayers family and blamed them for Viv's murder. This tit-for-tat action by John Henry was deemed to be a disguised two-fingered salute to those concerned.

This certainly seemed to nullify Watson's so-called assisting the police with Viv's murder. Secretly swearing away every top crook's life could, in reality, have been a ploy to save his own skin. He seemed to forget that he was a suspect in the Viv murder inquiry in 1994, and when he was in Gateshead Magistrates' Court on 12 March that year he said to the police and the Crown Prosecution Service (CPS): 'Why don't you fuck off? You couldn't catch us for the shooting of Viv Graham.'

John Henry, as this author predicted from the day he was arrested, walked from that court in Leeds a free man, acquitted of all three counts of violence against him. The CPS were said to be banging their heads against the wall over his acquittal.

Mickey Dixon, unbelievably, was found guilty of conspiracy to cause grievous bodily harm, and received nine years. He was the saddest sight to see. Unwittingly, he used a mobile phone he had bought and eventually given back to Tony Leach and he also stole a car! Dale Miller, the supposed gunman: not guilty of murder but found guilty of manslaughter ... 16 years. Eddie Stewart admitted his role as getaway driver: not guilty of murder but found guilty of manslaughter ... 13 years.

The finale came on 2 October 2002 when the Honourable Mr Justice Douglas Brown, a decent sort of judge, vacated Watson's plea of guilty to murder and accepted a plea of guilty to manslaughter ... 11 years! Twenty million pounds of taxpayers' money down the drain!

All of that supports what the hitman said: 'They'll think they can do anything now and that'll be their downfall. One of them will do something way over the top and get collared for it and you can bet they'll drop the killer right in the shit.'

In October 2002, Tony Leach faced a second trial. Having been cleared the previous month at Leeds Crown Court of the Freddie Knights murder, he now faced charges relating to arson, burglary and damage attacks. It was claimed that Leach had been the evil mastermind behind attacks carried out on businesses in the North from Yorkshire to the Scottish Borders.

As in the Knights trial, Leach entered a plea of 'not guilty'. The prosecution claimed that he had hired henchmen to carry out attacks on the properties of various businesses, including restaurants, take-away shops, car dealerships, a pub, a hotel and a seaside caravan site, causing a total of £1 million worth of damage. Charges were brought against Leach of conspiracy to commit arson, burglary and criminal damage between August 1999 and December 2000.

A key figure in bringing about the prosecution case was self-confessed arsonist Stephen Kingston. He was arrested when police investigated the murder of Freddie Knights, and during the course of police interviews Kingston admitted carrying out attacks on property. Leach was named by Kingston as the principal instigator of these attacks.

Top QC William Taylor urged the jury not to be taken in by Kingston and went on to stress the benefits that Kingston wished to gain by turning supergrass, which included a new identity, a lenient sentence for the part he played in these property attacks and, of course, a new life under police protection.

On 28 October 2002, Tony Leach was cleared of all charges relating to racketeering. Having already been cleared of the Freddie Knights murder, he was free to walk from the courts, his first taste of freedom in over a year, as he had been held on remand.

The supergrass system has been proven not to work. Supergrasses failed in the Knights trial, as they failed in this trial, which must bring such tactics into question. The ease with which someone can be charged borders on the insane, especially when criminals are relied upon in the witness box.

7

STARTING OUT

To find out what made a man such as Viv tick, we need to examine him from a much closer perspective than an outsider's point of view. Below, Sharon Tate, the sister of Viv's fiancÈe Anna Connelly, gives an insight into Viv's everyday domestic life, but it would be wrong to assume that those closest to him would reveal anything in terms of skeletons hidden in Viv's cupboard.

'I knew of Viv,' Sharon recalls, 'when he was a doorman at the bottom of Shields Road. There was trouble there at that time and he just seemed to come on the scene from nowhere. At that time he wasn't very well known and the people knew he wasn't from this area. I think because of that he wasn't liked; he was from out the area ... Rowlands Gill. People were saying things like, "Who's this?" and "Who does he think he is coming across here telling us what to do? He's not from this place." So they didn't like him!

'He wasn't from the town, he was from the countryside, he just came in and started telling people they couldn't get in the bar because they were "worky tickets" [troublemakers] and they weren't getting in to cause trouble ... the town changed for the better when he was around.

'I knew him before Anna was seeing him in 1986. We would be having a drink in the bar and things like that, when he would come up and buy us drinks, so I got to know him a little bit. As time got on, Anna started seeing him and that was it.

'When it came to spotting trouble, Viv could definitely see where the trouble was and if he was there that was the end of it. One word from him and that was it!

'He wasn't a townie, but you wouldn't say he was a fish out of water, although I would ... because I knew deep down that he was green as grass through the way he would treat people and the kind of person that he was.

'He was really soft; he really wasn't what they were making him out to be. But he ended up exactly what they made him. But I don't think he was the kind of person that everybody thought he was.

'They built him up, they came and said, "You can do it." He could use his fists and he could do it, but that wasn't what he was there for. He was only there doing a job and just maybe seeing that they would drink up. "Drink your drink up, lads, howway!" There's loads of people who do that sort of job, and then he just seemed to get bigger and bigger and bigger.

'Obviously, if something did start and he had to fettle them, they could see what he was capable of and how quick he moved. He could handle ten people at once if need be, if it come that way. There's not a doorman in the town that could do that. He could do that because he was a boxer and was like a proper fighting man with his hands in that kind of a way.

'Whatever Viv's dad said, he did. If his dad said, "Don't go there, son. They're just enticing you there as their backup" or "They want to use your name", then Viv would take it all in. This would be voiced over many a thing.

'People wanted Viv to go to Spain as their backup in timeshare scams. His father, Jack, would say, "Don't you get involved, son. You keep away from that."

'Viv would go there for his breakfast and he would talk to his father while his mother made the breakfast and they'd ask what had been happening and they'd [Viv and maybe a friend] just have the normal crack. There was never fighting talk; his father would never encourage him by saying, "Go on, you do this."

'He would just say, "Keep away, son, nowt to do with you, they're just using you."

'Viv would listen and say, "Aye, father, you're right."

'And he would come back and say, "My father's told me to keep away."

'He was quite green, if you would say that was green. I liked what he did because you respected the way he did it. He never, never took liberties with people. I've seen doormen do things and I've looked and thought, Because there's two or three, look how they treat people.

'You never got that from him because he would come and he would say, "Howway, lads, howway!" and do it in a nice way or whatever. Even if he was approaching them, if there was trouble he would say, "Howway, lads, there's no need for this," and do it in a nice way. He wouldn't run in knowing what he could do with them in two seconds. He wouldn't run in and do it; he'd give them the benefit of the doubt. I liked the way he did it. He impressed me because I thought he was a gentleman and in the job he was in he did it in a nice way.

'From when I first met Viv up until his death, I saw changes in him. In the end, he would hardly ever go out. He would watch videos and ring us up and say, "Anna's making something, do you fancy coming across at teatime?"

'They always had their tea on time because Viv trained twice a day. His last training would be around about, maybe, seven, so Anna would have the tea on for him coming back. They would maybe ring here and say, there's chicken or whatever – do you fancy coming across, we've got a good video.

'We would join them for a meal, and then the next minute the video would be on, we'd be in the middle of our tea and then the phone would start.

'Viv would say, "Anna, what am I going to do?"

'He didn't want to pick it up because he didn't want to ruin the night, but he knew in the back of his mind he had to pick the phone up because he had to make sure people were all right wherever they were ringing from.

'He'd say, "Two minutes, two minutes. I'll be back in two minutes!"

'He'd run and jump into the car and he would be quick. Maybe he'd be 10 minutes or maybe 15 minutes and he'd be back and sit down and say, "Right, sorted, let's ..." and then we'd start watching the film again and the phone would ring again and this is how the night constantly went on.

'As for getting videos and for sitting in with Anna, that was all he really wanted at that time. I'm talking about two years before his death, but prior to that they had their good nights out. Being out late, maybe clubbing, and that sort of thing, but the last two years he didn't even want to go out. He was happy with his videos.

'I think that Anna did him a lot of good because he must have felt happy. His relationship was steady and he was happy with everything that was there. Probably the pressure was a little bit too much at the time and he was glad to just stay in and not be anywhere where things were happening.

'There was still the likes of Rob Armstrong and all of them still placed in all the clubs wherever Viv would work. Even then, he didn't really work in them, but he knew that if anything was ever said it was always said in his name: "It's Viv Graham you've got to face."

'So, although Viv was sitting in the house, this news always reached him.

'Maybe Viv would get a phone call the next morning saying that two kids were in the previous night acting themselves and stirring up trouble, saying they were going to do this and so on. Viv would know it would be put down to him, type of thing. Even though Viv wasn't personally in attendance he still had his finger on the pulse.

'Viv used to get splitting bad heads; he suffered them on a near-permanent basis in the end. Viv and I used to laugh because we were like two hypochondriacs, both suffering headaches and thinking the worst.

'He used to take me training with him and his headache would come back and we used to say, "Here we go." We did suffer the same things. I had an abscess and had to have it cut out, then he had an abscess and had to have it cut out.

'I used to complain and say, "I'm sure I've got a tumour!"

'Viv would reply, "So have I."

'He was always complaining about bad heads. When you

get an abscess you're run down – it's one of the signs of being run down – so it was getting to him, but you would only know it by him saying he had a bad head.

'Near the end, he was getting phone calls saying they were going to take his life, but he just used to laugh because he had heard it that many times before. Maybe the first four or five times he'd maybe have been frightened, but after a while he'd heard all what they were going to do to him.

'Viv didn't care about his money. Whatever money he had he spent! David, my husband, would try to get Viv to do something with it. He'd say, "Howway, Viv, do something with it because at the end of the day you're going to get older and somebody's going to come along and knock you out."

'We used to laugh about it.

'He wasn't cared because he lived for the day and he'd say, "I'm not bothered."

'David would say, "I'm going to get you a lovely diamond ring because you should be wearing a nice ring. You should have a nice watch and a nice house because your job isn't easy, so you should have something that you can say is yours because of what you're doing!"

'David went and got him a nice ring and he loved it. Viv was over the moon. He didn't ever get himself a watch, but at the time Viv had said he wanted somewhere nice for Anna to live because Daisy Hill [in Wallsend] was a bit rough. They loved it there, the people loved them and they loved the people, but David wanted him to do something because he knew Viv was a waster with his money.

'He said to Viv, "You've got to get something under your hat because you're getting on."

'This is when they started looking around at little places.

David was behind him, pushing him into things like that. Nobody else really thought about these things, everybody was only seeing the other side of him. Having a drink, having a bet, doing this, just squandering. David wanted him to make something to put behind, but Viv always said, "I'll never see 40, man. Live for the day, I'll never see 40."

'And now, when he hasn't reached 40, you wonder what was going on in his mind. He said to us all the time, "I'll be finished, me. I'll have my leg blown off; something'll happen to me before I'm 40. I'll not see 40."

'So obviously something was ticking around in his head telling him that.

'He used to talk about what he should have and what he'd got and I'd say, "Look at the life you've got to live, what have you got for it?"

'He didn't confide in us about any trouble. You would never hear him. He knew he could handle it, but it was only his bad heads that he would complain about.

'It used to gut me. I felt like seething because people didn't even know him. Rumours about Viv would get out of hand. It would go from one week into the other and the next minute he'd done this and done that, and it used to hurt me because I used to think, if they only knew him, if they knew the type of lad he was, they would think the world of him, they would have loved him. Because he was genuine and he was a gentleman in every way, even in the way he sorted his trouble. I respected him for the job that he was in because it wasn't an easy job. The way he did it, he made it look easy.

'I remember we were in a nightclub, it was pitch black and we were right at the back. Anna and me were there and Viv was leaning on the bar talking to us, then he just shot from out of our sight. Then I just saw him: he had this man held right up in the air by his neck.

'I was saying, "Eeeeh! He's taking liberties, look at the size of that little man." I said to Anna, "What's he doing that to him for? He's never done a thing. I'm going to tell him."

'I went across towards where Viv had this man. I saw this lass screaming; Anna was saying to the lass, "What's happened, what's happened?"

'One minute Viv's leaning on the bar talking to us and then the next minute he's got this lad up by the neck. Anna thought the lass was screaming because Viv had her lad up by the throat. It turned out that the lad had a knife up to the lass's throat. Viv had seen it from where he was in the pitch black!

'That's how unbelievably quick he was. He grabbed the lad and took him to the door, where the doorman was, and he says, "Look at this? He was in here and he's had that knife. He got past you with this."

'He took the knife off the lad and kicked him up the arse, kicked the lad out and said to the doormen, "I'm warning you that you'd better make sure that people are searched properly!"

'Some time before this, when Viv was approaching the end of his three-year sentence for an attack on fellow club doorman Stuart Watson, an incident happened in a nightclub. A sex pest in the Studio nightclub glassed a young woman after she had slapped him. The young lady died from the result of being glassed in the throat. Viv had this on his mind when he spotted the same potential fatality that could have happened here, the same nightclub where the glassing incident had taken place. Doormen were supposed to be searching people for weapons and had obviously slipped up. Viv was none too pleased with them.

'The lass said to Anna that the lad had a knife held to her throat. The lad was her boyfriend, but she'd chased him off and he wanted her back, so he was threatening her. The lass was in the toilet with Anna and had been telling her that the lad had been threatening her and he would do this, that and the other to her and she didn't think he would be in the nightclub that night, but he was. The lass was very thankful for the way Viv had reacted.

'Viv had an uncanny knack to spot trouble and get people out of tight spots. It was as though Viv could read what people were saying by just looking at them. I used to flinch when I could see that Viv had spotted trouble. But you could look and see nothing happening, and then you would see him stepping back and making his way to wherever. The next minute a fist would be thrown. He knew what was going to happen before it actually happened.'

8

SUSPECTS

During the night following Viv's murder, Wallsend Police had received a number of anonymous calls informing them who was behind it. Being informed and being able to prove it were two entirely different things, as they were to find out. The police investigation centred on piecing together a picture of Viv's business interests and his associates. The forensic team were quick to act on this high-profile murder and had the crime site cordoned off a short while after Viv was taken away to hospital.

A post-mortem was carried out the day after Viv's death, so no time was lost in establishing the cause of death: severe haemorrhaging caused by gunshot wounds. A coroner's inquest was held and Home Office Pathologist John McCarthy said that Viv had died from gunshot wounds to the thigh and abdomen.

Anna Connelly and Viv's mother, Hazel, did not attend the

hearing, which was adjourned for a date to be fixed by Brian Gallon, the coroner for South-East Northumberland. This meant that Viv's family could not make funeral arrangements until the coroner's court had completed the inquest.

Viv's last hours on that fateful New Year's Eve were pieced together by detectives. In the morning, he was at home before travelling to see his parents at Highfield, and then he visited his childhood sweetheart, Gillian Lowes, who lived near them at that time. He returned home and just after 2pm friends called at the home he shared with Anna and her two children to wish him seasonal greetings. He then called at Anna's parents' home nearby.

Afterwards, he drove to Wallsend in his Ford Sierra Cosworth and parked in his usual place in Border Road, off High Street West, around 4.15pm. What happened from that time onwards has already been set out.

Viv felt secure in the East End of Newcastle. He was well liked by the publicans in Shields Road and Wallsend High Street, part of a main road that continues eastwards into Howdon and North Shields. He was the publican's first port of call if they ran into trouble with pub goers who were intent on causing trouble. Men felt safe to go out for a drink with their girlfriends or wives. Viv took the fear of trouble and crushed it up in powerful hands that could just as soon express his tender and caring side when people needed help with paying their bills. He was a soft touch for the odd sob story, and that set him apart from the typical hard man without a heart.

The usual hard man is the bully who at school picked on those he knew he could dominate and then carried the habit into street life as he got older. But there is hard and there is rock hard. The rock-hard men were those who worked relentlessly in the shipyards, men capable of lifting steel girders weighing more than twice their body weight.

There had to be some skeletons in Viv's cupboard that could be pulled out and shown as proof that he really was a bastard to his family and was the mastermind behind the '£2-million drug empire' often linked to his name – an empire that never was, of course, as Viv was fiercely opposed to drugs. What other reason could there be for his being killed? Just another hard man being put six feet under, some would say. Who was going to miss the likes of him?

Viv had undeniably been tainted by city life and this was reflected in some of the things he did that raised a few eyebrows, but there was nothing that could not be explained away. Looking into Viv's cupboard for skeletons was like looking for a needle in a haystack, for with Viv it was a case of what you see is what you get. He had a few vices, but nothing that he was shy about. Had he tried to cover up his notorious gambling, fair enough, it would have been a revelation, but he made no secret of it.

He did not, as people thought, have a stash of cash. Every conceivable method of looking into his past has been used and a book could be written just about that. Nothing was revealed that he would have been ashamed of. He did not kill anyone, although he nearly did when involved in a fight, but he paid the price for that. He did not use weapons on anyone and people always knew he was fair and would listen to what they had to say. He did not like to pay his debts: believe it or not, he used to hide behind the door when the man called to collect payment for the TV. The three-piece suite was bought 'on the drip' and Viv's car was 'on the chucky' [both hire purchase], so where were all Viv's millions? Maybe it was a bluff: get the car on the drip and it would make people think he had nothing. That was not the case, though, because he really did not want the taxman on his back. After all, he paid enough betting tax on the horses, as he was a big layer of bets; but more of that later. He did not play his cards close to his chest when it came to gambling.

The police team investigating Viv's murder started looking at case files from other killings, hoping to find a connection. Every conceivable permutation was examined. Sixty-five police officers were involved in the investigation, which meant some routine work had to be put on hold. High-profile policing was brought into play and uniformed officers were strategically placed in town-centre pubs until publicans had a new Pub Watch Scheme in place.

Detective Chief Inspector Keith Felton said that one of the difficulties of this sort of inquiry is that 'people are afraid to come forward' with information. Detective Superintendent John May said that the killing created a 'power vacuum' on Tyneside. People were indeed frightened to offer information, but a lot of intelligence was gathered by the police in and around pubs and clubs that Viv had watched.

Wreaths laid at the scene of the shooting were moved by an unknown hand – a bizarre act that served only to provoke more anger. Neither the police nor the council accepted responsibility for the disappearance of over a dozen wreaths and bunches of flowers that went missing through the night.

The police called a meeting of those who were alarmed about what could happen in the wake of Viv's death. Superintendent Eric Mock, the Wallsend area commander at the time, said the meeting was to enable the community to discuss the town centre's problems, which had been highlighted by Viv's murder. 'It will give me a chance to put people's minds at rest a little,' he said.

Within a month of the murder, the police had arrested five suspects in dawn raids. In the circumstances, it was good police work and intelligence gathering had helped a lot. There were lots of people willing to talk, but only off the record and some only over the telephone.

Viv was a well-liked man in and around Wallsend and in the end that worked to the benefit of the police investigation. People had lost their beloved Viv and those responsible for his death would be informed on one way or another. Such a response was not the norm in this hard, inflexible anti-grassing area.

The police were starting to build up a picture of what might have been the killers' motive for striking in such a grim fashion. Five people were arrested in late January 1994 and questioned under caution about the murder while detained at Wallsend Police Station. One of those allegedly arrested was Alan Wheat, 32, an ex-boxer living in Northwich, Cheshire, who had connections with those held in Wallsend.

The only woman among them was an ex-shoe-shop manageress from Wallsend, 23-year-old Karen Young. Two of the four males arrested were Brian William Tait and Darren Arnold. After lengthy questioning, two people from the Wallsend area were charged with drug offences and appeared before North Shields Magistrates' Court the following day.

The former boxer from Cheshire was released on bail, the only one out of the five who had not been charged with an offence. Detective Chief Inspector Keith Felton had applied to the court for an extension to allow the police to hold Karen

Young and her boyfriend, 29, for further questioning. Karen's father Alan Young, 55, another of those arrested, was charged with possessing a stun gun and further drug offences.

News had leaked out that Karen Young was one of the five suspects arrested. She was soon on the receiving end of some sinister deliveries. One was a black-magic-type doll that had been made into an effigy with its eyes pulled out; another was a wreath bearing the message: 'See you soon, Viv.'

Late-night and early-morning threatening and malicious telephone calls were received at Young's home. She said that her life had been ruined since it was found out that she had been arrested with four others in connection with Viv's murder.

Two men from the West End of Newcastle were arrested in early-morning raids in March 1994. They were questioned about the murder at Wallsend Police Station, and held for over a day before being bailed out without charge. Intelligence had been gathered on the two suspects for months, but the police stressed that the men were arrested as part of an overall strategy to uncover further details in readiness to bring charges against a number of people for their part in the plot to murder Viv Graham. It was obvious at this point that a number of people must have conspired to kill Viv, and the police were now getting the infrastructure into place so that they had an airtight case against those they now suspected.

One of the men detained for questioning was wanted for a number of other crimes and for failing to appear in court, as well as facing extradition to Switzerland. Lee Shaun Watson, 23, who lived at the Ord Arms pub, in the Cowgate area of Newcastle, had outstanding warrants for assault on a police officer and drink-driving. He now faced a trip across the Tyne to Gateshead Magistrates' Court to face those outstanding charges; he was given unconditional bail and the case was adjourned for three months, but he was immediately arrested by Gateshead Police.

Next, Watson was taken to Bow Street Magistrates' Court in London, arrested on an extradition warrant and again remanded in custody, charged with the robbery of a jeweller's shop in Zurich in which over £300,000 worth of cash and jewellery had been stolen in August 1993. He faced a total of four charges, including two of robbery, in connection with the theft in Zurich. There was a brighter side to Watson's situation, though: he faced no charges in relation to Viv Graham's murder and was eliminated from that inquiry. Watson's record of violence includes a jail term of seven and a half years he was handed in 1995 for the series of armed raids he carried out on jewellers in Switzerland. He was also, subsequently, jailed for 15 months for a stabbing attack and possession of a butterfly knife. And, as we saw earlier, in 2002 he was sentenced to 11 years in the Freddie Knights case.

More than 350 statements had been taken from witnesses; that was a lot of paperwork to sift through and it was done from a small operations room quite unlike the new one, with its up-to-date technology, that is now in use. Considering the rudimentary facilities, the police worked well. Over 1,000 people were spoken to officially in connection with the murder, and many more unofficially. The police were using the HOLMES (Home Office Large Major Enquiries System) computer, which, to some degree, could cross-reference the information they had gathered and fed into it.

In April 1994, the murder inquiry was considered to be

draining police resources and most officers were deployed back to their usual duties, with only about a dozen continuing full-time inquiry work. The police obviously considered that they had collected enough information and that this was sufficiently strong to give them a case. All they now needed to do was cross the Ts and dot the Is before making their submission to the CPS.

This had been a very thorough police investigation. One illustration of their diligence: in October 1994, ten months after the murder, they acted on information that led them to believe that a Rover car abandoned in Monkton Lane, Jarrow, South Tyneside, had been used by Viv's killers. The car was taken away to be checked, even though links with the killing were tenuous; it was thought that a dark Rover had been seen trying to get into the lane that the stolen blue Ford Escort was blocking while waiting in the back lane off Wallsend High Street just before Viv was shot; or that a car of this description was carrying associates of the killers, who were checking if everything was all right on the run-up to the murder.

In January 1995, the police were ready to pass on their files for the attention of the CPS. After all their work, it looked like the police were ready to bring charges of conspiracy to murder, among other serious charges, against a number of people who had been interviewed in connection with the murder. The hard part was over now and all the police could do was wait for the CPS to get back to them. The fact that files were submitted to the CPS meant that the police were satisfied that they had discovered those responsible for the killing. But had the procedure been followed to the letter?

May 1995 saw the CPS advising that there were no

charges to be brought against the two men and one woman still on bail facing charges of conspiracy to murder and other serious charges. The CPS had spent four months studying the files of evidence. It was now nearly a year and a half since Viv had been murdered.

The top and bottom of it was that there was insufficient evidence to bring charges, said the CPS. Allegedly, it was also said that defence barristers could demolish some of the witnesses by assassinating their characters since they had criminal records. Looking at it from this angle, it can be seen that the CPS were perhaps right in advising there were no charges to answer. For, if the killers had been charged and got off in court because the case against them was flimsy, the police would not really have been able to pursue them at a later date should more evidence have come up.

A date could now be set for the full inquest into Viv's death. The last day of June 1995 saw the start of the full inquest into the murder. Club doorman Terry Scott, of Westerhope, Newcastle, had made a statement to the police in which he said, 'I saw Viv in the street; he was lying in the gutter facing me. As our eyes met, I knew it was serious. He kept repeating, "I'm going, I'm going", as I held his head.'

The coroner, Brian Gallon, recorded a verdict of 'unlawful killing'.

He had released Viv's body in early 1994, and after a burial certificate was issued in March of that year the delayed funeral service could go ahead.

9

FUNERAL FOR A FRIEND

The family had decided to hold the funeral service in St Patrick's church, near Viv's childhood home. They had, however, underestimated the esteem in which people held Viv. He had touched the lives of thousands of people, while others who had just heard of him were intrigued at how such a man could be so loved.

Despite the family's appeal for a low-profile service, many people felt that they were close enough to Viv to warrant their attending the church, and about 1,000 mourners turned up. Some people do not get to know that many people during their whole life, yet this was just the core of people who would have attended had an open service been allowed.

There was no memorial service, but such an event would have filled a cathedral with those fiercely loyal to the memory of this profoundly loved man. The most faithful would have changed places with Viv without hesitation if it could have brought him back. As mourners surrounded the church, it looked like the killers had underestimated the strength of the following Viv had built up over the years.

The tiny stone-built church of St Patrick, in High Spen, has a capacity of only 150. One of those churches that would not be out of place on a picture postcard, it has a little steeple and small leaded windows that make it look welcoming to those who seek sanctuary there in their time of need. The 100-year-old church was big enough to serve the needs of the local community, but never before had it been host to such a huge, or notorious, gathering.

All those in the church that day, whether believers or not, had been called to a place of worship to pray for the soul of Viv Graham. Some of those present would not have seen the inside of a church since their christening, but had now set foot on to the turf of someone with an even greater following than the man they had come to 'see off'.

It was as though some of the mourners were from a secret brotherhood that came together only on such occasions. Armani suits, suntans and Rolex watches, mandatory items of eye-catching fashion, announced that those wearing them had made it big; manacles and shackles that showed that they had made it all the way to the top. Viv had no desire to be a materialist. His car was his only possession that meant anything to him and even that was expendable if need be, just a tool he used to get to places in a hurry. People relied on Viv turning up fast and his car afforded people the comfort of knowing he would not be too long about it. People had suggested to him that he buy himself a nice watch or some jewellery so that he would have something to show for his money. In the end, he bought himself an expensive ring, but, although he wore it, he did not feel it represented his having made it in the world. He was a humble man who thought nothing of giving someone the price of a meal if they needed it. However rich or poor a life any of the mourners lived, it was not for anyone in the congregation to judge how Viv had lived his.

Among the mourners were Viv's father and mother, Jack and Hazel, and the three women he had relationships with: Anna Connelly, his fiancée; Gillian Lowes, Viv's childhood sweetheart and long-term lover, who had two children by him; and Julie Coffell/Rutherford, another of Viv's past loves, who also had two of his children.

A double-decker bus was used to transport mourners from the East End of Newcastle. Aboard were pub landlords and regulars on a mission to show the unity of their feelings about the loss of such a man. Local people were also among the mourners. Villagers had seen him grow up and to them he was simply Viv, the local lad murdered in Newcastle. They only knew him as a happy-go-lucky person who loved his children and animals. Two very different cultures bonded in a common purpose: to say farewell to Viv Graham.

As a child, Viv had been on the receiving end of a thumping or two in children's squabbles when he was just a 'bairn' living in the locality. Those who did the thumping were now here mourning. How could anyone want to shoot their Viv?

Numerous cars made up the cortege and the hearse, at their head, was packed inside and covered outside with floral tributes. The humble home of Mr Eric 'Jack' Graham and his wife, Mrs Hazel Graham, was the starting point for the cortege's short journey.

Viv's parents' modest but comfortable semi-detached home was a far cry from the sprawling city streets of

Newcastle, which were jam-packed on Friday and Saturday nights with people intent on having a good time. The house, on a council estate in Highfield, would always be Viv's first love, even after he made a new home in Newcastle with Anna Connelly. Viv's idol was his father, and this relationship reflected his loving upbringing in a family that held traditional values. Hazel, Viv's mother, used to cook cakes and other goodies for him and, on his daily visits, she would slip them into a bag for him to take back to Newcastle.

Today, though, they were burying their son. All the things that had been good about life had become unimportant to them, apart from their grandchildren, who gave them just enough reason to hang on to sanity. They could now lay their son to rest some three months after he had died. That brought them some relief, but the crowds of people and cars parked all around the church were a daunting sight. Despite this, the occasion passed serenely, and Viv would soon be resting in the cemetery where he used to lay a wreath every Christmas on his beloved grandmother's grave.

Traffic police were used to guide cars off the main road and among the mourners were police officers involved in the murder inquiry. The beautiful Derwent Valley, in rural Northumberland, to which tourists flock in summer, was witnessing an intrusion into its spring awakening, but there were no complaints from the close community about this brief disturbance to its calm, for one of its sons was being honoured.

The coffin was lifted out of the hearse with the help of Viv's father, his brother and Peter Connelly, who, among others, acted as pallbearers. The Reverend Martin Jackson led the service and in a moving eulogy said that words had been spoken after Viv's death that hurt people, words that should not have been said. Viv was a big man with a big heart, he said.

Mourners were asked by the vicar to pray for Viv as he went on his last journey to the grave and to remember him with thanksgiving before God.

One important remark by the vicar summed up what Viv was all about: 'Viv helped break fear in a society which is gripped by fear, not just publicans, but also elderly people and children as well.' A man of the cloth was saying that Viv had sorted out the problem of fear.

Viv's eldest son, Dean, then aged eight, attended the service with his mother, Gillian Lowes. Dean was supposedly the only child of Viv's at the service, but Julie Coffell had brought Viv's daughter, Jodie Ann, to the service.

The Reverend Jackson read out a story written by young Dean that said: 'He loved everybody. Even if they had done something wrong, he still loved them.' It went on to say that Dean and his younger brother, Viv junior, loved being with their dad. The story is moving and you can imagine this 17-stone ex-boxer, a man of raw, muscular power, sitting his son on his knee and saying how he still loved those who did wrong.

Tina Turner's hit 'Simply the Best', an anthem among the boxing fraternity, was played during the service. This touching song echoed through the rafters of the tiny church, bringing suppressed tears to the eyes of tanned Tenerifans paying their last respects to a comrade before returning to Spain's island of timeshare-touting dwellers.

Plainclothes police officers mingled with the mourners, hoping to hear things of interest that might shed some light on a murder that was yet to be solved. The mourners sang a favourite hymn of Viv's: 'On a hill far away stands an old rugged cross …'

After the service, the mourners moved to the local cemetery to say their prayers as the coffin was lowered into the ground. Gillian Lowes collapsed with grief on seeing this last organised goodbye.

The mourners who were specially invited to the service attended a wake immediately after the graveside ceremony. Highfield and Rowlands Gill Working Men's Club was the venue for this celebration of Viv's life; a last accolade to Viv that would show solidarity among his close friends. Jack Graham had to dig deep for fortitude to help him through the ordeal because it would not do for the father of *the* Viv Graham to be seen to break down. Nor would Viv have wanted to see his idol in tears. Gallantly, big Jack managed to get through it. His son was now a sleeping giant.

Hazel Graham warmly greeted the mourners in her motherly way and thanked them for coming. Among the mourners there would have been some who were intent on avenging Viv's murder; an 'eye for an eye'. There was trouble in the packed Queen's Head, Viv's former haunt on Wallsend High Street. The police had received information that guns were going to be used in an attack to avenge Viv's murder, but a raid yielded no more than a replica gun in the possession of one of the pub's regulars, who claimed it was only used as a deterrent to defend himself.

Near the end of Viv's life, most of his professional responsibilities lay in the East End of Newcastle. He was responsible for the Bigg Market and Quayside areas, in the centre of the city, only if he was specifically called on to go there. It would be easy to say that Viv 'scudded' the undesirables first, but that was not always the case. As often as not he would give a verbal warning and if they did not take heed of that he would look at the situation afresh. Just as the police issue a caution, so Viv would offer a warning; and the next time the wrongdoer would be charged.

Where did all of Viv's mates go, with their so-called allegiance? Viv was a part of Newcastle, he made it a better place in many respects, and those who would denigrate his character do so only because he is dead and cannot defend himself. Yes, Viv slapped people about, but most of those who have been on the receiving end of a crime – whether it was being burgled, having their car damaged or even their washing stolen off the line – would want to do the same to those responsible.

No matter who these victims thought responsible for the crime, it was often not appropriate to grass them up to the police, either because it was not in their nature to get someone into that sort of trouble, or because, if they did so and the criminal found out, they would be victimised and face even more trouble.

The best alternative was to see Viv, who would go and find out if the suspect was in fact responsible. If so, the situation would be remedied, and not always with a slap, as he usually gave them a more conciliatory option. In short, he fixed problems that no court in the land could resolve. This was zero tolerance, instant justice – Viv style.

10

VIV'S HAREM

Viv had a plentiful and abundant love life. Three main women, and more besides, were involved in his tangled love life. Right to the very end they were combatants in a bitter fight to gain the proceeds of insurance payouts. Julie Rutherford, Gillian Lowes and Anna Connelly were the three women in Viv's harem.

There was no other woman in Viv's life – just other women! Viv used to call Gillian 'Little Lowesy'. When they were at school, they had pet names for each other. Viv used to call at her home and complain of terrible headaches, having gone there directly from Anna's. Gillian put these headaches down to the pressure of his work and not to the boxing, which some people thought was the cause. But how could she know about Viv's work, when she admitted that she did not really know what he had to do to earn a living? For a woman who said she was in the dark like this, she certainly knew plenty about what he got up to in his work. Everybody wanted looking after by him, she said, and it really got out of hand and in the end he could not cope. 'In the last year of his life he was receiving lots of threats and he was really stressed out.'

Gillian also said that Viv took these threats seriously, and for some reason she assumed that someone had rung him from London to say they were coming up to Newcastle. Viv did, in fact, confide in her about a threat he received from London and said that because of this she had to stop taking the Pill – it is difficult to tell if this threat was something he had invented to get Gillian to stop taking it because he wanted her to have his baby. He liked it if his women were pregnant, as it made them unattractive to other men. Maybe all his outward machismo had made him feel emotionally stunted inside and not sure if he could trust anyone. Maybe people had made him empty promises in his formative years.

And perhaps his headaches, which could be taken as a sign that he was mortally ill, were another ploy to get Gillian to come off the Pill. Whatever the truth, Viv asked her to stop taking it, and to her that meant he must have received a threat that he had been expecting. But her response was to tell him there was 'no chance' of her coming off the Pill for him.

If Viv really loved her so much, why did he use every male trick in the book to ditch Gillian when he was invited to go abroad? There was one occasion when they planned to go to Cyprus for a break, Viv having been nominated to be best man at a friend's wedding there. But, when Viv told Gillian that he did not like going abroad, the trip was scrapped.

To make up for this, Gillian booked a holiday on her own

in Corfu. When Viv found out, he tried to dissuade her from going, but ended up taking her to the bus station so she could get to the airport. Was this to make sure she was going on her own? A few weeks later, and without Gillian, Viv went off on a holiday abroad.

A place that Viv seemed to enjoy taking his conquests to was Blackpool. He took Gillian and another couple there, and as soon as they arrived Viv was off to the betting shop with the other man in tow. So desperate was Viv to get away and have a bet, he didn't even stay to help get the suitcases out of the car.

The other woman whispered to Gillian that Viv had won a lot of money. Viv denied he had won anything at all. Gillian recalled, however, that she patted his pockets, looking for the money, and the next day found about £500 hidden in a cushion. She went mad at him. If Viv had thought more of his women, surely he would have flashed his cash? Clearly, Gillian did not believe Viv when he said he had not won any money. But why did he conceal this information from her?

This contradicts what Gillian had said earlier about Viv telling her everything. If that was the case, why did he not tell her about his win? The difference between Viv and Gillian, which she admits, is that he did not value money. So why did he hide it from her? For obviously he was concerned enough about her finding out about it to secrete it away.

At the time Gillian was having Viv's first child, he was off seeing Julie Rutherford. Gillian did not want to become pregnant, but she came off the Pill anyway after deciding she no longer needed to take it because their relationship was at an end. But, even though they were no longer together, she and Viv started having sex again. The result was that she became pregnant and had a baby son, Dean.

Viv said to Gillian that he would not live with her but would come home when it was all over. What was he waiting for to be all over? Gillian did not expand on this, but her talking about it suggested she had an idea of what it was.

Viv confessed to Gillian that he did not love Anna Connelly the way he loved her and that she would always be his childhood sweetheart.

Gillian recalled Viv coming back from one of his holidays. 'It was about six o'clock in the morning when he called with a suitcase with three bottles of perfume in it. He said that one bottle was for his mother, but his mother did not ever get it, so it was obvious he had bought each one of his three lovers the same bottle of perfume home from the holiday!'

During that visit, Viv proposed marriage to Gillian and she wrote down his words so as to confirm what he had said. But it was not to be, and she was kept hanging on, as were the other two women.

Viv went off with Julie while he was still seeing Gillian, who was gutted to lose him to another woman. Gillian must have felt second best to Julie, as Julie must have felt second best to Anna when Viv moved on to her, leaving Gillian third best.

Julie was all over Viv like a rash when they first met, in Finnigan's bar in Gateshead. Gillian noticed this and became very jealous. Viv was promptly thrown out, along with his eight carrier bags of belongings. He stayed at Gillian's only a few nights of the week as he was still living with his parents then.

Anna commented on the fact that she used to send clothes to Gillian, but in retaliation Gillian said, 'Well, looking at

Anna's taste with that horrible yellow dress, what does she look like in that!'

Viv, now seeing Julie, said to her, 'Whatever happens in the future doesn't count, doesn't matter.'

Julie, having had a few halves of lager, asked, 'What are you talking about?'

Viv again said, 'Whatever happens in the future doesn't count, this is a new beginning from today.'

Julie takes up the story:

'I was going, "Yeah, yeah, yeah, right."

'Little did I know at that time that he had been with Gill and obviously she was pregnant and he didn't have the bottle to tell me. I didn't have a clue and then I think we fell out in the September for a while and he was going away on holiday. He said he was going away on business and we ended up having a big huge fight and he went.

'My friend was there and she had seen it all. He was on the phone to her from the airport and whinging on and then he was ringing me, saying that he had made a mistake and this and the other, and he came back. It was just before my birthday, in the September. He was sitting in front of the house, looking up. I was in a different house then. I looked out and thought, What's the matter with him?

'Because he used to come up and confess, I didn't want to hear things. He had come to confess; he said he had actually been away with Anna. It took him about two hours to tell me it all.

'I demanded, "Just tell me!"

'Viv countered, "No, because you'll leave me. Tell me you won't leave me."

'He wanted me to swear on my bairn's life that I wouldn't leave him.

'I prised it out of him. "Come on, you obviously have something to tell me."

'He half confessed, "You've already just said her name!"

'I just said, "Anna."

'And he went, "Yeah."

'I flipped!

'Then, a couple of days later, it was my birthday and it was crawly, crawly time. I went out on my birthday and he was locked up [in prison] that night, 29 September. He was actually locked up after twelve that night, because we had been out; he dropped me off, went to work and was locked up from there.

'Then, in December, he hit me with the news that "Gill had a baby". Prison visits are about 20 minutes, half an hour, or something. I think I made a lot of enemies at that particular time. People would come on the visit with me and I didn't want them on the visit because I needed to know what, where, who, why, how and everything. I think I was nasty to one or two people and after that I stopped going.

'I said, "That is it!"

'I wasn't getting anywhere, I phoned Rob Armstrong's wife and I said, "Will you tell Viv I won't be back, we're finished?"

'She went, "OK."

'I literally moved house and everything, but then he started to phone. When I went back, he said that Anna had been visiting and he told her that he wanted me to come back in to see him. By this time, it was about March. I had stopped going for weeks and weeks. I used to go about four or five times a week. I know his dad used to go on a Thursday and I would go most other times.'

Looking at what Julie says, it is quite clear that Viv was replacing the loss of Anna's prison visits with Julie's, as

Anna said she had walked out during a visit, leaving Viv with the engagement ring. Viv threatened to destroy the prison! Obviously he had a rethink and persuaded Julie to come back.

Anna said of Viv's second child by Julie, 'Viv always believed that this other man was the father of the child to Julie because Viv had assumed that his associate who he used to train with had accepted responsibility for the child that Viv had denied was his. Viv never seen his daughter [his first child by Julie], but I always gave Alan Rooney (a friend of Viv's) money and presents to take up for her.'

On hearing this claim, Julie retaliated, 'Well, I've got a 12-year-old daughter who can be asked if she ever seen her dad; of course she seen her dad. If Anna knew Viv, then how could she possibly be certain of what she says? Alan Rooney bringing me presents and money for my daughter from Anna is not true.'

Anna: 'I always sent Julie things, even Gillian Lowes, whether it was Mother's Day or even Christmas Day. Whoever you get to speak to you will tell you. If you ever speak to Rob Armstrong, he'll tell you.'

To this, Julie said, 'Tell you what? Well, I don't know where she was sending these things to, but she wasn't sending them here. Do you think I would accept presents and gifts from Viv's girlfriend? No thank you, I don't think so!'

By coincidence, after Viv died, Julie and Gillian were attending a solicitor's appointment in connection with his estate, and they spoke briefly. Julie was not comfortable with some things that Gillian related to her and later, in an interview, she felt the need to put her side of the story.

Anna stated that for Julie to become pregnant by Viv with

her second child by him, she would have had to have sex with him on a prison visit.

'It's true,' Julie said. She did have sex with Viv while on a prison visit and conceived their second child, Callum.

Seething on hearing this, Anna claimed that Viv knew Julie was seeing someone else: 'It wasn't a thing that bothered me. I said to him, "You did have sex with her and it could be [Viv's child]."'

Julie retorted to Anna's allegation: 'She's lying on that! I had never to go out, never mind seeing any other man.'

Anna: 'It wasn't a thing that bothered me because I hadn't been visiting him and he said, "Nah!" For some reason he didn't think it was his child; he knew Julie was seeing another lad. Viv used to say to her, "You want to get your maintenance paid for that bairn." Viv felt the real father was a man he used to train with in a gym who gave Julie a lift to prison to see him. Viv fell out with that man and went to train in another gym.'

Julie: 'Rubbish, the man was Viv's very good friend. There used to be two guys, one used to take me up to see Viv, but he used to aggravate things, because Viv was very, very jealous and he used to say stupid things to wind him up. Anything would wind Viv up. Someone might say, "I saw her knickers when she was getting into the car to come and visit you," and that was it! So Viv had said, "I don't want him to bring you in any more," because he was a wind-up and for other reasons.

'Viv had this other man bring me in, as he had Viv's car at times. I know that Viv had been told that the car had been seen outside my door at six o'clock in the morning, which was a load of rubbish as this man was petrified of Viv. The man that Viv's friend had said was at my house while Viv was in prison wouldn't even look at me from across the road. Who in their right mind would? Who would do it? Would I do it – be stupid enough to get pregnant by somebody else and face the wrath? No! I don't think so, that's silly,' said Julie, her voice drying up with emotion.

She had mentioned facing the 'wrath', so it was put to her that Viv was assumed to be a gentleman and if it was the case ... 'I would have emigrated, I wouldn't have done it,' she answered.

It was again put to Julie that Viv surely would not have been as nasty with her as she was suggesting he could be, especially if he thought she was pregnant by someone else. She replied, 'I think it would be a different kettle of fish if I had told him that I was going with somebody behind his back! Viv was a very, very jealous and possessive man. I don't think he would have took it lightly.

'I didn't understand why he wasn't at Viv's funeral. Somebody had said they had a fall-out. Why did they fall out? I've never seen this man from visiting prison and I still don't know why they fell out.

'When Viv said, "You want to get your maintenance paid for that bairn," he would say that! In a joking manner.'

But what if someone else had said that? Would Viv have accepted that as a joke? Julie was asked. She had difficulty accepting this idea: 'If somebody had went in and told Viv that I was going with somebody else ... No, no, it's too stupid for words, nah!'

When Gillian had been engaged to Viv, everything was fine until she discovered he was seeing Julie and she then gave Viv his engagement ring back. This scenario is uncannily like the one in which his last fiancée, Anna, allegedly returned his engagement ring on a prison visit after she discovered that he was seeing Gillian behind her back and that he was the father of Gillian's latest child. This so much incensed Anna that she walked out of the visit and did not go back; in fact, it was Viv who went, cap in hand, back to her to beg her forgiveness and dedicate himself to being loyal to her again.

Anna says of this, 'Eventually I caught him out when he went to jail and one of the other two, Gillian Lowes, was pregnant. By this time we had just got engaged and just come back from our holiday. I had found out when she had come to jail to visit and someone I knew had seen her on that visit and they told me she was pregnant.

'I pulled Viv and said that Gillian was pregnant and Viv told me that she had got herself a man. He still wouldn't say it was him until I found out. I went to the jail and gave him the engagement ring back and I told him, "That is it!"

'He pleaded with me to listen, "Please, listen to me! I'll tell you the story!"

'I said, "No way."

'He said, "You walk out of this jail and I'll smash this jail up!"

'I said, "You best smash this jail up, because I'm away!"

'And I went. I got a letter sent from his mam to say that he had been full of drink that night [when Gillian became pregnant].'

(Author's note: Anna says she gave Viv the engagement ring back, yet Anna says they got engaged when Viv came out of prison on Mother's Day. Maybe they became re-engaged.)

Anna continued, 'I never went to the jail to visit him, but Gillian Lowes and Julie Rutherford had been to visit him. Julie already had one child by Viv and she claimed a second to be his, which meant she had to have had sex with him on

Images of a legend. (*Clockwise from top left*) Viv loved kids – here he is as the proud godfather and father. Viv shares good times with Girlfriend Gillian Lowes; in fancy dress; Viv loved to relax by going fishing; Viv as a young man; living the jetset lifestyle!; and pursuing his favourite sport, falconry.

Top: Always the life and soul, Viv lives it up with pals at the pub.

Bottom left: Viv with girlfriend Anna Connelly – at the time of his murder they were engaged to be married.

Bottom right: A hardman with a big smile, if you made a friend of Viv Graham, you had a friend for life.

This ramshackle shed called 'the hut' is where Viv put in countless hours of training at Highfield. The innocuous exterior contained the uncompromising machines of pain that made Viv so hard and fit.

Stuart Watson (*top*), the club doorman beaten up by Viv. Graham received a prison sentence for the attack. John Henry Sayers (*bottom*), a true man of honour who was wrongly implicated in setting up the cowardly murder of Viv Graham.

A force to be reckoned with. The legendary streetfighter Richy 'Crazy Horse' Horsley sometimes needed to be sorted out when he was getting too out of control. Viv was the man for the job.

The murder.

Top: Viv left the Queen's Head pub (*far right*) after a pleasant few drinks with pals.

Bottom: The back lane where Viv's killer hid and fired his deadly shots from.

Inset: A makeshift cross marks the spot in Wallsend at which Viv was senselessly killed.

Top: The plaque donated by well-wishers had to be removed after being vandalised.

Bottom: Another casualty of violence, Viv's nemesis Lee Duffy was killed in a knife fight. The pair were to have met in a winner-takes-all fight.

Viv Graham – simply the best!

a visit for that to be his child. Viv loved his children and I think that, if he thought that had been one of his children, he would have accepted it as his, but for some reason he wouldn't have that.

'I said to him, "But you did have sex with her and it could be [your child]?"

'After he come out of the jail, he came to me and said, "Will you come back to me?"

'He had sent me letters and cards and that. I said to Viv that he was a single man and he could do whatever he wanted and to go with Gillian or to go with Julie and whomever he wanted, but he didn't want this, he wanted me.

'We were going to get married and we got engaged on Mother's Day. I said, if he came back that would have to be the finish with Julie and Gillian and he couldn't have the one night away here and there because that's not what I wanted. I wanted a proper relationship. He loved my children and they loved him.'

Right up until the day Viv died, he was sneaking off into Gillian's arms. Gillian said that he did not keep anything from her and obviously this meant that, while she and Viv were having these secret meetings, she knew of Anna's position in this tangled situation.

While Viv was in prison, Gillian and his family were all friendly and acted like a family by visiting him as a group. Julie, though, stopped visiting, and so did Anna, which left just Gillian to receive his attentions. She is said to have laughed at the memory of having been the only woman out of the three to continue to visit Viv.

During Viv's imprisonment, Gillian had given birth to young Viv and a number of people connected to Viv called at the hospital to see the newborn baby. A man close to Viv at that time, 'Dodgy' Ray Hewitson, took some photographs into prison so that Viv could see his newborn son.

Gillian knew of the existence of Anna and Julie, yet she continued to meet intimately with Viv. As for Anna, she thought that Viv was only calling to see the children when in fact he was sneaking off to see Gillian. And both Anna and Julie did not know that Viv was still seeing Gillian behind their backs.

Gillian asked Viv why he did not want to live with her and the children. Viv avoided answering her by telling her to wait until everything was finished. He used the excuse that she or the children could get hurt, but in reality he was living in Newcastle with Anna and her two children, so that argument goes out of the window, as there was more chance of something happening in Newcastle than in a little village with only one main road leading into it. It sounds like Viv was stringing Gillian along with his characteristic tactic of 'keep them hanging on and pregnant'.

When it was put to Julie that Viv had begged Anna to take him back, she said, 'I've heard it all before. I've heard the same lines when I was pregnant and Viv liked getting you pregnant, but he didn't like having the responsibility of the pregnancy, certainly not. I threw him out actually when he went back to Anna.

'We had a fight, because my house was nearly burgled and it was because he was late, so of course I went off in a tantrum and we ended up falling out. He came back the next day and he got the alarm fitted and then obviously he went back over to Anna's and came back weeks later, but then I wasn't interested, but it was all right [with him] because I was safely pregnant and you were safe for nine months. Nobody is going to fancy you for nine months.'

Did Viv feel that after the pregnancy he could return to Julie? 'He came back, yeah. You are his possession. *You are his possession!* That's exactly what you are, until he says different. He didn't want to lose anybody, he didn't want to lose Anna and he didn't want to lose Gillian and he didn't want to lose me!'

Viv was reasonably honest with Gillian, but how honest was he with Julie? 'He wouldn't have dared!' Julie said. 'He was obviously open with Gill, but not with me, no! Obviously I knew that he was living with Anna. He used to come and confess, but that was after I had Callum.

'He was Anna's, because she could have him as far as I was concerned, but it doesn't stop you loving him. And I loved him and I still love the man, but I hated him at the same time. I knew for a fact that he was living with Anna then, but it didn't stop him from coming here.'

So Viv had never made up his mind and said he was going to live with Anna? 'Not likely! He had every excuse in the book.'

It was explained to Julie that Anna had said that Viv had no time at all to be able to have trysts with Julie or Gillian. Julie's response to this was: 'If she could keep an eye on him, then she's a better woman then I am.'

As far as Anna was concerned, Viv did not have time for such flings, as he was always on the mobile telephone speaking to her. He would be back from wherever he was within a short time and he would bring Anna her cigarettes because he did not like her going to the shop for them.

Julie's comment on hearing this was: 'I wasn't even allowed to go to the ice-cream van.' Was Viv frightened that she would run off with another man? 'I don't know,' Julie answered. 'I just know he knew I wouldn't do it. Viv was dead for some time before I considered going out again. He was definitely insecure within. There was one night I went out and he was here at eight o'clock in the morning! My female friend and I had been out and we were lying in bed laughing and carrying on when he opened the door. He was just standing there because he knew I had been out the night before, which was when he was with Anna. Anna was, like, saying, "He's my sole property." Anna is silly because she knows that's not true. *It's not true!*

'There was a mutual friend of ours and he used to phone every day even when Viv and I weren't speaking. He phoned her every single day. It came to the stage where I stopped going to her house until after he died because she told him everything, what I had on, where I was going and everything.'

Viv's affair with Julie resulted in two children. Gillian said that DNA tests were being carried out to establish that the second child Viv had with Julie was his and that Viv's parents were not co-operating with this as Julie's solicitor had contacted their solicitor. Gillian gave the history behind the name of Jodie Annie, Viv's daughter by Julie: the name is Viv's grandmother. (Author's note: Since this wrangle over DNA tests, it has been accepted that Viv fathered Julie's children Jodie Annie and Callum.) Gillian went on to say that she had babysat Jodie Annie and that the child was all right but she had wanted to do so no more than occasionally.

Queen of the Castle seems to be what Viv made each of the women in his life, and if the worst came to the worst he put them in the tower, so to speak. By getting them pregnant, he made them less attractive to other men and in this way he felt safe to devote his time to the others.

Gillian felt on cloud nine to know all his intimate secrets, secrets that none of the other two women knew, and clearly the fact that their relationship was clandestine made Viv more attractive to her. She asked Viv not to lie to her, but his favourite saying to her and to each of his other women was that he felt relaxed in her company and that her home was like a sanctuary. That sanctuary, however, would last only a short while, for Viv's watch was his master and time made him hurry to his next appointment. 'I've got to fly now, bye,' he would say.

Gillian accepted that she was one of Viv's harem and she went along with all he demanded of her. She said that Viv used to hurry off faster to the bookies than anywhere else, but he always rang her and he was never off the phone, calling at all times of the day and night. Was he checking on her whereabouts?

If she went out, she would return to find Viv had left messages on the answerphone demanding to know where she had been and why she had not come back home by 11 o'clock. He would be at Anna's or Julie's place and she knew that to call him there would have caused problems. Gillian had somehow turned from being Viv's childhood sweetheart – he had 'acquired' her by winning a £5 bet with a fellow pupil that he would kiss her – to being the 'other woman' in his life.

But she was determined not to lose her grip on Viv, even though it would have been easy to let him go and make of her life what she could. She wanted him regardless of his lifestyle and despite the fact that she had become his second choice.

Anna Connelly claimed that, when he died, Viv had not arranged any financial allowance for Julie's children because he had assumed that the associate that he used to train with had accepted responsibility for the child that Viv denied was his.

Julie's view was: 'Load of rubbish, load of rubbish, that's maybe what he told her.'

But then why was Viv in a state of denial about this child? Julie answered this by saying, 'He just told you what you wanted to hear; he was the same with me. I'm not saying it's the coward's way out; he just didn't answer you, he just didn't like to hurt your feelings. If that got him away with it then he would say it. If Viv had admitted that he was the father of our second child, then Anna would have had a fit, wouldn't she? That's probably what he thought anyway.'

Was Julie and Viv's relationship over with after she had Callum? 'Well, it was over for that time, but it was on and off all the time. That would be it for a couple of weeks then he came back in about the March and I was getting ready to go out and I didn't really see him much after that, but I used to keep in contact with him and he would call occasionally.

'He had paid for me to go on holiday, Primrose Valley, the four of us [Julie and her three children] in a caravan. I have an older son and two little ones, and I went off with my cousin and I never heard from him until the Christmas. Viv had sent the money for us in 1993.

'He phoned me from hospital [where he had an abscess lanced]. I had never been on holiday with the little ones; he asked where I was going.

'"Caravan."

'"Yeah, that's OK."

'So he sent me some money over via taxi. When I come back, that was it. I never rang him. If he wanted me then he knew where I was.

'Then he sent Robbie Warton at Christmas. He was gone in December; I had not been seen going out with him in the last two years of his life as he said, "It's too dangerous. You wouldn't believe the lifestyle I've got now, Julie."

'He came here and it seemed he had the world on his shoulders. He knew it was his sanctuary and he knew he was safe.'

Viv told Gillian the same thing – that he feared for her safety – yet he was living with Anna almost in the heart of Newcastle! If he felt threatened himself, what made him stay where he felt all the more vulnerable in that his fiancée and her two children could be got at? Perhaps he used this argument about safety to keep Julie and Gillian hanging on a thread, available whenever he wanted them and on his terms.

Julie quoted directly from one of the many letters that Viv sent her while serving his three years in prison. In it, he wrote that the only way he would be out of danger was to get shot dead. 'But,' said Julie, 'it might just have been an excuse, as the man was full of excuses. The last two years of his life were totally different to the time we spent together, totally different.

'The exact words Viv wrote down are: "The job I do, you don't know when the fuck you could be killed ... Julie, from what you've heard today you will see I live a dangerous life the only way I can get beat is by getting shot."

'That was letter number 134, written on 11 June 1990. This is what he wrote when he was in prison, but his life was different when he left prison. The last two years I don't know what happened.

'Yes, I know people used him. They always did, though; he was too nice. Viv's father said they used Viv as a money box; that's exactly what they have done.'

Did any of Viv's supposed friends ever give Julie any support? 'Oh yes, they've asked, "How are you?" and that was it.

'I made a lot of enemies when Viv was in prison, they used to think things. This friend of Viv's has a lot to answer for as far as I'm concerned. He used to say to Viv, "She's working herself again!"

'I used to get letters from Viv and he would say, "I don't want anybody but you to come in." That included his friends. He would say, "I love my friends, but I'll see them when I get out." That is the way Viv was. His friend would say, "It's her!" And so I was the villain of the piece.'

Was this man's friendship with Viv under threat? 'Definitely. I was the scarlet woman by the sounds of it. I think he did the same to Viv's dad. Viv had said that I couldn't put right the damage caused where his dad was concerned.

'I would say, "What are you talking about?" I don't know what he said. I hadn't ever spoken with Viv's dad. I was a threat to this man. He wanted to be the closest to Viv.'

But somehow this man and Viv had a falling out? 'Well, exactly, I had said that to Viv's dad at the funeral. I said, "Wouldn't you have thought that after what he had done to you that you would realise the things he had said about me were lies?"

'He would say, "I know, I know."

'My one and only concern is my son and what people have said about him. Viv just wasn't the same guy. He used to always be happy-go-lucky and couldn't give a monkey's. He didn't and wouldn't involve me in his private life. I didn't open the door to the press. I was just put down as Viv's secret love and I just let them get on with it.

'They had my name down as "Coffell" in the papers. I let

them get on with it, I couldn't care less what they said, I wasn't reacting, so I thought, dead end. Anna had made me react to this because of what she had said about my children.'

Anna alleged that Alan Rooney brought presents from Anna because at that time he lived near Julie. Julie: 'He brought the little one's car, a Noddy car, and he fixed it up. It was his birthday or something. Robbie Warton brought a big tractor and a couple of buggies; it was when Viv was banned from driving. Viv would phone and say he was sending them over; they never came when he didn't tell them to. Viv did not like me to have money; he thought if I had money I would go out. If we weren't speaking, then he would not give me money.

'When I first met Viv it was in Finnigan's bar, at Felling, in Gateshead. Viv actually nipped my derriere; he wasn't as suave as people would believe. He wore a pair of Crimplene trousers and a fly-away-collar shirt, but he had the charm and he had the smile. Apart from that fact, he had a lovely bum. He nipped mine, so I had a little bit more to drink and then I nipped his. Apparently he was with his girlfriend, Gill, and she had seen it and it had caused an argument, that's what I remember from it, and from then on that was it. We were an item for years and years as far as I was concerned, until he was murdered.'

Of her fiancè, Anna said, 'Viv was an organised and neat person; he would even get the vacuum cleaner out. He wasn't a very good cook, though, but he could do egg and chips. If I wasn't very well and he made a meal it was egg and chips. If we went to his mam's, she always had a dinner on the go, one for each of us; she knew I wasn't a very good cook.

'Viv could be timed; he would take my children to their school and then he would leave time so that his children would be in the playground at their school in Rowlands Gill for, say, 11 o'clock. He would visit his children in the school playground for five minutes and then go straight to his mam's. [So Anna thought!] I could time him. Because after he had died it was suggested that he had been seeing Gillian behind my back. I don't know where he got the time from because he was never off the phone to me, ringing me from his mobile telephone soon as he got to his mother's. If I needed cigarettes he would say, "I'll be there in ten minutes. I'll get you them."

'I couldn't go to the shops. I couldn't go and visit friends, they had to come and visit me. That was the only bad thing about him, the jealousy. That wouldn't have happened if we didn't go out and had stayed in. Sometimes I would think, instead of going out, just stay in. I don't mean every time when we went out, it just depended on what I wore. I dropped the short things and went into long dresses after that.

'I could never go out with the girls and because of that he couldn't go out with the boys either. If he said, "Can I go out with the lads?" I would say, "All right, but can I go out with my sisters?"

'He would say, "No!"

'I would say, "Well, you're not going, then."

'He was over the moon and would then say to his pals, "She'll not let me go out."

'He wouldn't let me go, so I wouldn't let him go. His friends would twist their faces. People used to say, "Wherever you see Viv, you see Anna, he never leaves Anna; the two of them are constantly together."

'If I went to the toilet, he would wait outside the toilet

door, everybody knew that. People used to say, "He's outside the toilets? Oh, Anna must be at the toilet."

'If I was in any longer than five minutes, he used to open the door and shout, "Anna! What are you doing, who are you talking to?"

'He didn't like that; he used to ask, "What were you talking about?"

'I would say, "What do you think I'm going to do? You know how much I love you. I'm never ever going to leave you, we're so, so happy. So why is it you act like that?"

'I used to think that because, maybe, he had been sly with me by going with them [Gillian, Julie and others] and telling me lies and then, when he was sent to jail and came out, he knew I had never ever been with anyone. I've never been with anyone since the day he died or ever lived with anybody, so he knew what type of person I was. So I thought, Maybe he thinks I'm going to do back to him what he did to me and this is his insecurity with me.

'He said to me, when I gave him the ring back on the prison visit, "You'll love somebody else."

'I said, "That's one thing I'm not going to do, go with somebody just to pay you back for what you've done to me. That's just not my style."

'I wouldn't do that, get a man and think, Well, he'll be sick for what he's done to me. So he knew I wouldn't do that. I think he had this insecurity where he thought I would like to do back to him what he did to me, that's what I thought, anyway.

11

GAZZA LIFTS THE LID

Ever since Viv's death, there has been conjecture about who was behind the horrendous injury Paul 'Gazza' Gascoigne suffered to his knee when he was assaulted in Newcastle city centre. Rumour had it that Viv was the attacker.

Gazza's career has brought him riches beyond any normal Geordie boy's belief. Who would have guessed that, when he was playing football for Redheugh Boys' Club in Gateshead, he was heading towards international stardom on the hallowed turf of Wembley?

Gazza might seem like a lovable rogue on the surface, but underneath he is a very complex and sensitive man, and, although you might not think it, he does not suffer fools gladly.

When Gazza agreed to grant an exclusive interview to the author of this book about something as emotive as the nightclub incident in September 1991 that caused further injury to an already damaged leg, it was deemed an honour to take up the cudgel on his behalf.

How easily Gazza's words could have been twisted and sold on to a national tabloid. One thing stopped that happening: this author assured Gazza that nothing he said would be twisted. That guarantee still stands and will maybe restore some of Gazza's faith in writers. His private life could be probed in fine detail but it would not be any different to many people's lives; unless, that is, the press were to get hold of something that they could magnify into a story they judged to be newsworthy.

The minute Viv was dead, someone came out of the woodwork and claimed that it was Viv who was responsible for the attack that almost wrecked Gazza's career when he punched a Lazio player to the floor at a Newcastle nightclub. A supposed friend of the dead Viv is credited with saying this. With friends like that, who needs enemies?

In fact, Viv did not have many friends; not unless you count hangers-on as friends. His real friends were people who had very little physical prowess. He loved talking with old people and gave them the reverence they deserved. Children always brought a smile to Viv's face and when he smiled his teeth were as white as ivory and gleamed like diamonds. For his friends, too, he always had a mile-wide smile that could often put things right for them, for at times that was all it took, just a big smile. Viv did not need to prove anything or go about jealously guarding his territory like a king penguin defending his square metre of ice.

The attack on Gazza at Walker's nightclub in Newcastle came just before his £4.8-million transfer from Spurs to Lazio. It was claimed that Viv couldn't stand the thought of someone as famous as Gazza coming to Tyneside with his own minders and the claim further asserted that, as far as Viv was concerned, Newcastle was his town and he was top dog. Utter rubbish!

The top and bottom of the story is that Gazza had been on a night out in Newcastle in July 1991 with his sister when, in an incident unrelated to the attack on him, a drunk bumped into her, causing some concern for her safety. Being the good brother Gazza is, he came to his sister's defence and ended up being charged with assault on two men. What else could he have done? Anyway, Gazza faced criminal charges after one of the men decided to press charges because he thought he could earn money from the publicity that the incident would inevitably generate.

The assault on Gazza in Walker's occurred after he and friends had been to watch Newcastle United play Derby County at St James' Park. They made their way to the nightclub via a few pubs, in search of some respite after a tiring day.

Gazza's leg was recovering from ligament trouble and a fellow player from Tottenham FC was also recuperating from ligament surgery, and along with a group of friends they hoped to round off what had been a pleasant day out by visiting a nightclub in Gazza's native North-East.

This is what Gazza said about Viv Graham in order to end, once and for all, the speculation about the attack made on him in Walker's: 'It has been claimed that an attack made on me in September 1991, while I was in Walker's nightclub, was carried out by Viv. This had been reported in the press as having happened because Viv "couldn't stand someone as famous as Gazza coming to Tyneside with his own minders".

'I didn't go anywhere with Viv in Newcastle and when

visiting Walker's I was in the company of a fellow footballer who played with me at Tottenham. We were both recovering from ligament trouble. In the company were some local friends and my brother.

'I can say with certainty that Viv did not attack me nor was he present when the attack took place. Viv found out about the unprovoked attack on me and telephoned my good friend Jimmy Gardner on his mobile. Jimmy passed on Viv's concerns, which were meant in a protective way. While I appreciated his concerns, I passed a message back to him that I wanted the matter dropped and Viv respected my wish. Jimmy was not there with me as my minder, he's my very good friend.

'People were bitter about me leaving Newcastle at that time, so I stopped visiting Newcastle and invited Viv to visit London for a night out and a drink with me. This didn't happen but the invitation was always open.'

There you have it direct from Gazza; no twisted words or lies from a dead man's associate or friends. Gazza did not need to go to the trouble he did to put the record straight. He understands the grief this episode must have caused Viv's parents. Viv idolised Gazza.

The injury that Gazza suffered in the nightclub attack caused a fracture to his right knee and he was whisked off to a top hospital, the Princess Grace, in central London. Meanwhile, the police were trying to identify Gazza's attacker, but then word reached them that Gazza wanted the inquiry dropped and was not pursuing a complaint of assault.

Strangely, nobody witnessed anything of the attack on Gazza! Bouncers on duty saw nothing, staff saw nothing and Gazza himself would have been the last to see anything. For the attacker made a cowardly move in which he got right up to Gazza from behind, called out his name and, when Gazza turned around, knocked him to the ground with a blow to the chin.

Our own enquiries revealed that a lot of people thought the attacker was Michael Sayers. This seemed possible as he and his brother Stephen were into drug dealing and needed to have access to all the nightclubs in Newcastle, where no one dared to turn them away from their door. However, those who blamed Michael Sayers for the attack were his former associates, and this casts a different light on the accusation. It was all too easy to blame a man who, at the time of the accusation, was locked away serving 12 years for demanding money with menaces.

We have ruled out one man, but we cannot name the man who did make the attack. That is not because we are frightened to do so, but simply because we were not given his name. However, two reliable sources have come up with the same scenario implicating the same man.

This man was in prison, bragging about the attack to our informant, saying that he was off his nut when he attacked Gazza. He ran over when Gazza had his back to him, shouted at him and then threw a punch that unbalanced him, knocking him to the floor. When Gazza was on the ground, his attacker started jumping up and down on him, not knowing what he was doing. The assault was over as fast as it had happened and the culprit ran off into the crowd. He was not a big name, just a 'nobody' who fancied having a go at Gazza. An interesting question, though, is: where were the club's bouncers while this was going on? The regional manager of First Leisure, which owned Walker's, made enquiries but came up with fresh air as no one claimed to have witnessed the attack.

Viv had domestic arguments with his beloved fiancÈe, Anna. A hurtful remark can unleash all sorts of hidden demons and sometimes he would let fly and occasionally he would pull a door off its hinges, not knowing his own strength. Anna was never hurt, the damaged door would be replaced soon enough and the two of them would have kissed and made up before the sun set that evening. Viv was venting his rage on an inanimate object, but at that time he was taking steroids to increase his bulk; and with very good reason, when you consider that characters like Lee Duffy were looking to have a fight with him.

This tendency to fly off the handle is a characteristic that Viv and Gazza shared. Yet this spontaneous reaction has led to their reasonable side being overlooked. In fact, both gave money to just and good causes. And both, when faced with sensitive issues, exemplified the 'new man'. Viv thought nothing of vacuuming the carpets at the home he shared with his fiancée Anna. Gazza would grab a camera from young adoring fans who called at his home when he lived with his parents and reverse the situation by taking a shot of them. A rising star who had just got into Newcastle United's first team, he was still unassuming enough not to realise his celebrity status among the public. Viv had similar adoration from many people and it took some time for it to dawn on him, too, that he was a celebrity of sorts.

Celebrities and underworld figures have always had an affinity and a kinship. In the UK, the Kray family were perhaps the first to bring the worlds of stardom and crime together. Suddenly they were in the limelight as much as the stars they hired, and they became the celebrities.

The likes of Tim Healy, one of the stars of the BBC TV hit series *Auf Wiedersehen, Pet*, would visit Newcastle's nightclubs and mix with all sorts of nefarious characters, even if unwittingly. In one story, which is told by a person who was very close to Viv, it is alleged that Healy got involved in a fracas that had nothing to do with him.

Viv was a very possessive person and when he was out with his fiancè he would watch her like a hawk because there was always some Casanova waiting to pounce on a stunning head-turner like Anna. In Julie's nightclub one evening, Viv had cause to visit the men's room and on his return he spotted a man leaning over and talking to Anna. He read the man's lips and knew he had said something intimate to her.

Lip-reading was something Viv had picked up when, in earlier years, he had been a doorman working in an environment where loud music drowned out what was being said. He had to be able to detect trouble before it even started; reading people's lips gave him an edge.

Viv returned to the table where Anna was sitting and asked what had been said to her.

Anna, not wishing to have any trouble, said, 'Nothing, Viv, he was only asking if I wanted a drink.'

Viv shook his head and said, 'He was saying something else, wasn't he?'

At times like this, there was no arguing with Viv. This was his woman and he did not like the thought of her being propositioned like a common tart by some nightclub Romeo. That was how his mind worked: his woman was special and strictly off limits and he did not like it if other men cast eyes on her in a seductive sort of way, even if for a fleeting moment.

The man who had talked to Anna was near the bar with his friends. Viv went over to him and spat, 'That's my woman, you've been chatting her up.'

The man decided to have a go at him. Viv only intended to tell him where to get off, but the man thought he was about to be set on. Viv gave him a slap, which knocked his attacker down, and the others who were with the man were slapped about too, because at this stage anything could have happened and Viv knew you could not leave anything to chance. It was his environment and he felt at home handling this sort of situation.

Who should come innocently walking by, minding his own business, when all of this was going on but Tim Healy? According to Anna, Viv innocently thought that Tim was another friend of the Romeo he had just floored along with a number of the man's pals. Tim got a bit of a shaking, but nothing serious enough to bring his night out to a premature end.

Anna recognised Tim, but Viv was in too much of a protective state to be able to recognise the man he was shaking as a TV personality. Had he known that it was Tim Healy, Viv would have offered his abject apologies. Anyone can become innocently involved in someone else's troubles and it could have been anyone walking by; it just happened to be Tim.

Viv was a nobody, and then, just before he was murdered, he was on the threshold of becoming a minor celebrity. You can work for decades trying to make it big on the screen or stage with no result. Then along comes the media and, if they like what they see, stardom can follow in double-quick time. Get the right people in the right places to say the right things and you are in.

That is what happened to Viv. People who were already established in his field of excellence put in the word and he was elevated from country boy to city man. He still had to earn respect but he was halfway there and riding the tiger's back. There's an old piece of wisdom that says, 'He who rides the tiger can never dismount.'

Towards the end of his life Viv was starting to have second thoughts about his lifestyle, but he could not get off the tiger's back without becoming a victim of its wrath.

12

THE TAX MAN

We have seen how the connection between Viv Graham and Lee Duffy ran deeper than the disused coalmines of Northumberland and higher than Teesside's Transporter Bridge. Even so, Duffy had something about his nature that made Viv wary enough to keep him at arm's length. Lee Duffy didn't want to be upstaged by any man, no matter how big, and they don't get any bigger than Brian 'Tax Man' Cockerill. When the sun shines, Brian has to stand out of the way, otherwise the whole of Teesside is plunged into darkness.

Viv never had a face-to-face confrontation with Duffy, but Brian did. He tells the story: 'I was about 25 and Lee, the Duffer, was going by in a car. I'd just come out of a restaurant and, I always remember, I had my finger strapped with a metal splint because it was broken.

'Lee jumps out of the car with his mate and his mate's drinking a bottle of Pils and Duffy says, "What do they call you, then?"

'I thought he was going to say something like, "I'm Lee, John's told me all about you."

'Anyway I said, "I'm Brian."

'So I'm looking at his mate holding the bottle in his hand and, as I spoke, Lee hit me on the side of the head with his right hand and I see stars and I fall into a squat position. I grabbed him around the legs and he tried to push me away, but he couldn't, he didn't have the strength. I threw him into the wall and I headbutted him a few times and hit him with my forearm. I couldn't punch him because of my finger, so I headbutted him on the floor and he's shouting, "John, John, get him off me. Failey, get him off me."'

For the updated version of Brian's run-in with Duffy, buy his autobiography, *Tax Man* (Blake Publishing). This was the first time that Lee Duffy knew he had met his match in someone, and that someone was Brian Cockerill. If he couldn't beat him, he'd work with him as a collector of 'taxes'. In fact, Duffy had a few losses to his name from fights he'd had years earlier, but he was still developing his style and had some more developing to do before he would get to be a formidable fighting machine.

Together as a fighting team, he and Brian could have conquered the world but for Duffy's carefree ways, which included spending money on his friends like there was no tomorrow.

Others had an interest in Brian's fighting power and two in particular wanted to see a match between Brian and Viv. Brian recounts what happened: 'Stephen and Michael Sayers were willing to put £50,000 up for me to fight Viv and if it came off then they'd have been able to say, "We've got a better fighter than you now."

'I was in a rave club and I was talking to Robbie Armstrong, who was Viv's partner, and I'd had a fight with a big lad from Stockton the week before. I'd knocked him out and Robbie said, "Do you know a lad called Cockerill?"

'Well, of course, Robbie only knew me as "Big Bri"; he didn't know my second name was Cockerill. Robbie went on to say that the kid I'd knocked out had offered Viv Graham £10,000 to come and fight this Cockerill guy.

'Robbie said, "What do you think he'll do?"

'I said, "I think he'll beat him."

'He went, "He's that good, this Cockerill?"

'I laughed and said, "It's me, you daft cunt. I'm Brian Cockerill!"

'He exclaimed, "You're joking," and he couldn't believe it.

'About a week later, Robbie said, "Viv doesn't want anything to do with that fight, you know."

'I asked, "What fight?"

"Stephen and Michael Sayers put the £50,000 up," he replied.

'I didn't even know anything about it. What they were going to do was put a fight up in a warehouse in Gateshead or wherever it was, or Newcastle, and they were going to charge £10 a man to come in and watch it. They'd done all this behind my back without them even knowing.

'Robbie was saying, "The fight's supposed to be next month."

'I hadn't a clue what was going on. Anyway, I goes to Newcastle to see Stephen and Michael, I goes in the nightclub and they'd only invited me there because they knew Viv Graham was coming in that night, but he never come in. I guess they wanted a freebie, because they would have wound us up to have a go.

'I heard Viv did a lot of bad things with lads up in Newcastle; he invited Stevie Hammer out and then has a punch-up with him and punches him in the face. That for me was out of order, you know. When I was inside with Geordie kids, they used to say that he was a bastard for doing that. He'd get you up, get you pissed, put his arm around you and say, "Let's have our photograph taken," and then he'd punch them in the face; he was terrible for it.

'I remember how I met Sunderland's Ernie Bewick when Gary Robb had all the rave clubs and Ernie Bewick was brought down by him because I was in Stockton and Gary wanted to open a rave club there. I said, "You're not opening a rave club down here unless you pay me some money every night to open this club because it's my area, so you're not coming down here."

'The night had come for everyone to go to the rave club and I just told everyone not to go, so only about 20 people turned up. So the Robb brothers brought Ernie Bewick down to fight me, so I went down to fight this Ernie Bewick. I got there and we ended up shaking hands. He was the nicest person I've ever met, sound as a pound, great. I used to go and see him every weekend, up there in Sunderland.

'Ernie said, "I haven't come down for trouble, I'm just getting a few hundred quid on the door. It's your door, it's not my door."

'They were devastated because they had to pay Ernie a wage and they had to pay me a wage. They used to pay me £1 for everyone that went in. Because there were only 20 people in, they thought nothing of it, but the next Monday there was over 2,000 people in because I got all the kids to come then and it was a Bank Holiday and Ernie used to come down till about six o'clock. We used to mess about on the door with the [boxing] pads and things. The night he killed the lad, he phoned me and I said he should come down.

'Ernie had trouble in Sunderland when [David] Garside was brought in but they didn't fight. Ernie fronted him and then another time the Sayers come and they tried to beat Ernie, but Ernie had about 200 lads waiting in the car park – he had some pull in Sunderland.

'The Sayers didn't turn up when Garside was there because they were wary of Ernie. I knew Ernie and I knew them, so I was trying to sort it out. I was going up and I would go around the clubs with Ernie to meet the lads and that. I even met Gina G.

'Paul Ashton from Gateshead come into one of my clubs when I was in jail with his mate Monkey Lyons [Paul Lyons] – well, it wasn't my club but I was in charge of security – and he comes in and says that Paul's putting a wage away for me for when I got out; he was all right with me like that.

'Paul had a fight with Viv Graham and he was saying, "Fucking make him stand still," because Viv kept jumping around. Viv was only 15 stone at the time and Paul was over 20 stone. I was inside with Paul and he wasn't strong and I was curling more on the bar than he was benching. Paul could take a good shot on the chin, but he wasn't very clever with his hands.

'I remember when the armed police come for me because I was accused of having a couple of people shot in the town. About 17 cars full of armed police pulled up. I was in my car and I just drove off. They got me for dangerous driving but I said I was in fear of my life; they gave me two and a half years!

'If I never had another fight in my life I'd be happy. I entered the strongest-man competition but three days before I was due to go in for it I pulled my knee out. I often think it's not really worth doing because I'm all right on certain movements but when I run with the ball and pull the tractors it starts hurting. There's not much money to be made from it. Look at Glen Ross in Ireland; he's still working the doors and runs around in a little Fiat; he weighs 35 stone and he's got it wrecked.

'When I go out I try to be nice to everyone, but when Viv and Lee went out everyone would be frightened of them and they loved that. Lee used to love going into a club and emptying it and I think, What's the point of that? I like to talk to people and have a good laugh, but when I used to go into a pub with Lee it used to just empty.

'He used to give people a punch and I said, "What will happen is that one day one of those young kids you hit who's 18 or 19 years old now is going to be 30-odd and you're about 50 and he's going to give you a good hiding."

'Obviously he never made that age. The night he died, they were spitting on him and saying things like "Die, you bastard", it's true that. The lad up for his murder, Allo [David Allison], I beat him up after it; he never come out for six months after that.

'I remember me and Lee went to one dealer's house in Eston and there was about seven locks on the door and he said, "Big fella, get this door open."

'I kicked the door and my leg got stuck in it and he shouted, "It's on top, it's on top!"

'My leg's stuck in this door. That was his favourite saying and he'd wind me up into thinking the police were coming.

'He was a get for borrowing cars off people. He borrowed this car off a lad, a convertible, and he's going down to Middlesbrough, flying down the road, when he only goes and opens the hood! As we were driving it just blows off and blew away down the street and he just kept on driving.

'Another time we were in this car and it stalled at the lights. He said, "Ah, fuck it!"

'He just left the car at the lights, he done it loads of times. He used to take cars off people and just leave them in the middle of the town. It would run out of petrol, he wouldn't put petrol in, he'd just jump on a bus. He was mad.

'What I liked about Lee was that, after we had the fight in Redcar, some months later he come over and he sat and as he talked he gesticulated with his hands and he said, "You know that day we had the fight was the first time I knew I was beaten and for six weeks I couldn't believe I got beat."

'Some time ago a drug dealer was using my name for six months in order to protect him. He was saying that the heroin he was selling was mine. I took offence to how he was using my name because the police were starting to give me bother over it.

'The dealer then had the misfortune to be taxed for a lot of money [£21,000] and people suggested it was I that had taxed him. I then gets a phone call from his supplier and he said he wanted the money back off me and told me I was out of order. I told him to sling his hook, so he went to the best fighter in Darlington and he turned around and said, "What the fuck can I do with the big fella? I can't fight him!"

'He then asked who the drug dealer was and when he found out he said, "I wouldn't do it for him anyway because he's a grass."

'I remember when Peter Donnelly [of the Santino's restaurant attack] and Joe Hunt [ten years for robbery] tried to get me to team up with them. Joe Hunt's a nice lad. I had a rave club down here and he come down and said, "Are you all right?"

I replied, "No problem."

'I'd be in with every firm because everyone liked me and I got on with everyone, but some people tried to use me and they'd say, "You fight him."

'I'd say, "No, I don't want to do that."

'With Lee, though, he'd be off doing the fighting for others and that was the difference with him and me. People would get him into Newcastle and fill him full of Ecstasy and just have him running about taxing people. He might collect, say, three grand and he'd get one and they'd get the other two and it was him doing the taxing; he was just used really.

'I think what it was that, with Lee being in the jail for four years, he comes out and he was just enjoying himself being in all the clubs and everyone talking about him and he loved to have a fight every night so everyone would talk about it the next day; he loved that.

'At times, when I've had trouble, though, I've had to handle it differently. When Stu Watson come down here with Stevie Abadom, Stevie Hammer and all them, about 50 of them come down, a big busload of them and they come into one of the raves where I was and they all stood in the door and I shouted, "What the fuck are you doing in here?"

'I remember, Stuey Watson was sitting down, he didn't want to know. I went upstairs, come down. It must have been about 200 – we had all the Sunderland crew come down and the lads in the place – and I said, "If you don't go now, you won't be able to walk."

'They never come back. And it was some time later when I went to jail and they were all in there, Stevie Hammer, Geoff Brown and others and they were all right, we had a good laugh. Stevie Hammer was a nice lad. We used to sit in the passageway in prison playing dominoes and the screws would walk by when we were playing dominoes, looking at us as if we were mad.

'I've had guns pulled on me and you just have to confront people, "Come on then, you wanker." You know they're not going to do it; you just know when it's certain people, it's all bullshit. There was a lad here, Speedy, if he'd have pulled a gun out, he'd have shot you. He used to work with me and he got killed, he got shot. I was working it out the other day: there was about ten of us, all top fighters: Viv Graham, Lee, Duffy, Speedy and others; they're all dead or in jail.'

As much as Viv Graham was sought after to solve people's headaches when they were up against it, so was Brian.

The final story in this chapter goes to Richy Horsley from Hartlepool. Richy has also made his mark in the hard-man genre by virtue of publishing his autobiography, *Born to Fight* (Blake Publishing).

'Years ago, about 1992,' Richy recalled, 'I fought this big guy in a nightclub in Hartlepool; he was well known from a family of known people, and he used to run the doors in Hartlepool. Anyway, after he disrespected me for the second time, I called him on and done him. I broke his jaw, broke both his legs and also opened him up.

'I heard rumours that Viv Graham is coming after me, as the guy had paid him. Anyway, they told Viv that I was a bad guy and that I jumped him for no reason with a couple of lads and broke his legs with an iron bar. Pure fucking lies.

'Viv phoned someone in the town, and asked what I was

like, and the lad told Viv I was a straight guy and would never take a liberty with anyone. Viv said he had a feeling they weren't telling the truth about the lads and the iron bar and dropped it. There are always two sides to every story.'

13

POWER VACUUM

Newcastle was in turmoil: the top man had been murdered and who was next? Rival thugs were reported to be bracing themselves for a spate of tit-for-tat shootings. Any associate or friend of Viv had better watch out. One former close associate had made contingency plans by having a reserve car parked at the end of his street in case he needed to get away fast.

So-called friends had come forward and claimed that Viv had got involved in the drug scene in a big way and that he was blown away because he stopped taking supplies from heavy criminals in London. Viv had allegedly found cheaper drugs abroad. This was all baloney! Anyone with half a brain knows that the drug cartels of South America offer big discounts for bulk purchase. Where do they think the drugs originate? Apart from what is home grown in this country in sodium-lit gardens, in people's attics and lofts, the majority of drugs originated from South America. Now the drugs world is far larger and this lucrative trade is far more widespread, with other countries coming on the scene.

The same phoney friends of Viv no doubt knew the names of these London-based gangsters and helped the police out as much as possible when they made their enquiries into the murder of Viv. Of course they didn't.

The tension that hung around those associates of Viv in the wake of his death could be cut with a knife and also accounted for the scarcity of his supporters. But, in the area that he had adopted as his second home, Viv had become an unsung hero to many. At the murder scene, a plaque was quickly put up declaring: 'Uncle Viv, Our Hero, you will always be in our hearts.' Not an epitaph fit for a drug baron, for Viv was not one of these. The truth was that Viv had indeed been an avuncular figure to the many children who needed a man like him to look up to and to give them hope. Everyone has their hero and Viv was theirs, their very own local hero. Children are a good judge of character and have not yet lost their hope, their belief that all things are possible.

Accusations that Viv had been a police informer were now starting to do the rounds. Allegations that he had informed on crime families were widely reported. What is odd about this accusation is that Viv had served his three-year prison sentence for his part in the attack on a fellow club doorman, Stuart Watson. Do high-ranking police informers receive three-year prison sentences for committing violence that six pensioners, as Viv's father put it, could have bettered? OK, that was back in the early 1990s and maybe Viv had changed tack since breaking away from crime families and going it alone. Maybe he needed to survive by hook or by crook. If that was the case, he was not alone, since just about all high-ranking criminals use the ace card when the chips are down.

Viv was not party to any police covert operations against him and this suggests that, if he was informing, he was not passing on top-quality information. How likely was it that Viv would not have top-notch information at his hand to pass on the police? Someone claims to have spotted Viv meeting with a police inspector and a third party and believed him to be informing. It was confirmed that Viv was seen in Gateshead Police Station, but his car was parked in the main car park for all to see and it seems unlikely that he would be advertising his whereabouts if he had been up to no good. Northumbria Police spoke highly of Viv after his death. Would they have wanted to draw attention to their acquaintance with him if he had been a grass?

It has been suggested that Viv would still be alive if he had stuck to minding jobs and stayed out of other people's business and behaved himself like a good little boy. Viv did stick to minding jobs, because that is all that he knew, but that is not what got him murdered.

In December 1993, the month that Viv was murdered on Tyneside, a security company operating in the centre of Liverpool began taking over the running of club doors all over Newcastle. The company had previously only covered construction sites and retail outlets, but now it was moving into the big time. The company had had run-ins with the police. Other door-security firms had to be ousted and this was done by means of cash payments to doormen already in place. Not surprisingly, violence and threats were used against those who did not co-operate. Licensees were threatened with carefully planned trouble on their premises if they did not take on the company's services.

Newcastle was split into factions. No one wanted to take the mantle that Viv once held; no one wanted to be the next Viv Graham.

There was really only one man who could have replaced Viv as the supreme, heavy-duty ruler and that man was no longer around. As we have already seen, a Newcastle crime family wanted Lee Duffy to be a pawn in their game of chess and used him accordingly. They wanted to oust Viv from his empire. Such a scenario would have perhaps, if acted out, been a lifesaver for Viv, assuming he wasn't murdered at the fight venue. Viv was to have been murdered in the unlikely event that he won the fight with Duffy. The word 'unlikely' is used, as the majority of underworld figures on Tyneside and Teesside believe the Duffer would have emerged the winner.

A fine strapping lad, Duffy had made a name for himself in the Teesside area and could handle himself, as well as take a good punch. He lived with his girlfriend and daughter in an industrial area. He had had attempts made on his life, just as Viv had. Each man was no stranger to the threat of violent death and had been forced to stare it in the face at the wrong end of a shotgun.

When we seek to understand how the mechanisms used by the underworld fuelled Duffy's hatred of Viv we find a somewhat dull picture of betrayal and deceit.

In order to operate, drug dealers needed the support of hard men, but Viv was a thorn in their side. His territory, as a troubleshooter for publicans, was off limits to just about everyone. It was no use the potential drug dealer approaching Viv and asking him to stand aside and allow them to sell their wares. Instead, a plan was needed to oust him from his position of authority. There was no one in

Newcastle capable of doing this and, even if there had been, they would not have wanted the unenviable position that Viv held. The big dealers had to go headhunting outside the area in their recruiting drive for someone who stood a chance of winning a fight against Viv.

This was not a case of taking him out: he was too well liked and too high in the pecking order at this time. No, Viv had to be taken down a peg or two. Duffy was offered the opportunity to take over things in Newcastle, but there was just one slight problem: he would first have to beat Viv in a fight.

As we saw earlier, Viv did not turn up for the planned fight because he knew who would be there in the crowd watching and that, even if he beat the Duffer, he would be murdered. After Viv failed to show up for a second clash, Duffy, incensed, went around to one of Newcastle's nightclubs and started setting about doormen while wearing his fighting gear of shorts and a loose top. He assumed that Viv would see this as an insult and that it would provoke him to enter the delayed confrontation. But again it was no go.

Since Duffy's death, where are those friends now, those who would have used him for their own advancement and then tossed him to one side after they had brought him to Newcastle? How much support are they giving to Duffy's family? None! Supposing Duffy had fought Viv in Newcastle, and just supposing there had been an outside chance of his beating him, the tables would eventually have been turned on Duffy by his hosts. He would have become another statistic, one way or another. He would have become ambitious and, in time, would have become a threat to those who had brought him in for their own gain.

Looking at the other scenario, where Viv beats Duffy, it

would not have been as cut and dried as that because there was a faction dedicated to getting rid of Viv. It is likely he would have been murdered anyway: either killed by spectators with a knife or other weapon from behind while fighting Duffy, or shot dead at the end of the contest.

They would have been all over Viv like gremlins; they needed access to the East End of Newcastle at all costs, even at the cost of people's lives. Nothing mattered to these people. Viv had a family and friends, but in the end friends soon drift away, leaving relatives to grieve on their own. Had Viv not been so much of a loner in some respects, his following, which was big, would have known in which direction they were all headed after his death. As it turned out, it was like the blind leading the blind: great big men powerless to do anything, not even knowing what to do.

Duffy's death left a void on Teesside, as did Viv's on Tyneside, leaving what was called by senior police officer Keith Felton a 'power vacuum'. Maybe that was what was needed: the chance for the local police forces to carry out a thorough clean-up of the North-East.

Newcastle's East End, Viv's patch, was effectively even more of a no-go area for the big drug dealers, owing to the increased policing brought about by his death and to licensees fearing protection rackets in that part of the city. Getting rid of Viv did not have the desired results. Had the big players thought about it properly, they would have realised that no one would be able to replace Viv and the special kind of consideration that this country lad brought to the folk of Newcastle.

For, towards the end of his life, Viv did seem to take to city life like a duck to water. Yet, sympathetic as he was, he still did not fully understand the people and their ways. City life was not as straightforward as he thought. People held grudges and fought with weapons that could kill. Viv was like a village child trying to cross a busy urban motorway. The guidance he was given was wise, but it went unheeded.

'Fools go where angels fear to tread' would be too harsh a judgement, but it conveys to some extent what Viv was facing. Lion tamers should not turn their backs on lions, untamed or tamed.

Back to Stu Watson for his account of some of what happened after Viv was murdered: 'The main incident that happened in the Hobo's incident with Viv involved Rob Armstrong. Now, I don't hold a grudge, so, when Armstrong wanted to be in Rockshots after that incident, I let him back in.

'When Viv got killed, Armstrong got Viv's job down at the Venue [in Spennymoor, County Durham; closed after a fire]. He and Joe Hunt were working the doors. Armstrong stopped coming into Rockshots for some reason, but I didn't realise why until I went down there; it was me, Terry and Malcolm Faith went for a night out at the Venue.

'When I got there, one of the lads was standing with his arm across the door and I said, "Watch your arm!" I felt there was a bit of animosity there, a little bit of tension, and I thought, What the fuck's the matter with these? I knew some of the lads there because some of them worked for me at Rockshots at the time.

'I had a good night in there and the following morning, about 11 o'clock, I had a phone call from one of my friends and he said, "After you left last night, down at Spennymoor, Armstrong come in and they told me that you were barred and not to let you in."

'I reeled. "Barred! Not let me in? Why?"

'My friend didn't know why and went on to say that Armstrong was told, "If you want him kept out, then you tell him he cannot get in. That's not our job, we don't get paid to tell him he cannot get in."

'But I'm the kind of lad that, if I knew I was barred, I wouldn't have went because there was people there that worked for me, so I wouldn't have put them in a position that they needn't be in. After they finished at Rockshots, my lads would go on to work at the Venue and I said to them that I didn't want to see them lose their jobs over me.

'Armstrong was supposed to have sacked them all that night after he found out I'd been in. Joe Hunt was supposed to have come in at about 3am or 4am and, supposedly, he spotted me, went upstairs to talk to the owner and then he left. I wasn't aware of what was going on in the background. So the next thing I know is, I'm back at loggerheads with Rob Armstrong and I'm wanting to know why I'm barred.

'There's a pal of mine, Davie Zivvers, who was working around at Buzz on a Saturday night and it used to get full of shite, and he also worked at Rockshots. Davie tells me that this lad had pulled a knife on him and he said he'd be back on the Saturday night with a couple of lads. I said I'd come around with a couple of lads on the night. It got to about 1.30am and the kid never showed, so I said I'd have to go back round to check on the club to make sure everything was all right. I was just leaving Buzz and Armstrong come in and he tried to acknowledge me and I thought to myself, What a cheeky bastard after trying to bar me!

'So, when I left Buzz, Armstrong comes over to Davie Zivvers and says, "What's fucking Watson doing in here? It's not his club. That fucker tried to set me up in Cramlington [a village in Northumberland]."

'So there was kids standing there listening to what Armstrong had said and they couldn't wait to come and tell me; they set their necks to tell me what he'd just said about me saying I'd set him up. But they didn't realise what he was set up with.

'I said, "I saved his fucking neck up in Cramlington because Geoff Brown was going to kick the shite out of him at a boxing event held there."

'But he was with an ex-pal of mine, Stephen Vaughan, who's a big man with a big mouth who can't back it up. Stephen Vaughan, who was my pal at the time, was running about with Armstrong and Geoff was going to chin Armstrong, but I knew, if Geoff had chinned Armstrong, then Stephen would get wrong as well, so I stopped Geoff from setting about Armstrong.

'So Stephen was full of drink and drugs and he goes and tells Armstrong that he was getting set up at the boxing do and threw the shite in with it. Vaughan then started talking and telling tales out of school, but, if the truth was known, I saved Armstrong's neck.

'So on the Sunday, after doing the Saturday-night stint at Buzz, I went around the town [Newcastle] looking for Armstrong and during this time we've still got the flack going on with Terry [Mitchell] and [Paul] Ashton and now the flack starts with Armstrong.

'I seen one of Armstrong's pals on the door and said to him, "Get that fucking Armstrong on the phone and get him down here now. I'll fucking set him up. He got a bye the last time, but he's not getting a bye this time. Get him fucking here and we'll get it sorted out."

'So after Armstrong was phoned, I was told, "He's not coming down, he won't come down."

'I replied, "That's because he's a big useless cunt, that's why. He couldn't fuck off."

'He wouldn't come down to have a do with me and it was getting near Christmas, so we'd had a few drinks by the Sunday night. So on the Monday, we went off down to Sunderland to get the kids' rings for Christmas and I must have had a guardian angel looking over me because usually we religiously attended the gym for twelve o'clock, dinnertime, every day.

'There were 20 of them. They come into the gym with blades and knives and guns looking for three of us, but we weren't in because we were visiting Sunderland due to having hangovers from the drink.

'What had happened was, Armstrong had phoned Ashton up and said, "We've got a rick on with Watson and Mitchell and them."

'They joined together and come team-handed. Among them were Lyons, Ashton, Webber, Armstrong and some other doormen.

'So, when I found out about this, I phoned Armstrong up from my house and there was me, Kezza, Alan, Graham, Terry and Todd in my house then.

'I said over the phone to Armstrong, "Where are you?"

'His reply was: "Who's that?"

'I said, "You know who it is, you fucking puke! Where are you now? I'll come and fucking see you now, and me and you get it sorted before it gets out of fucking hand."

'He says, "I'm not going to fucking fight you, but Ashton will."

'I said, "Well, you come along with him and, after I've fucked Ashton, I'll fucking do you, you fat mug."

'He would not come and have a fight because he knew he

couldn't do it. He's never had a fight with anybody who can have a fight.

'Stephen Vaughan was there with Armstrong and I said over the phone, "Tell Armstrong to come on and we'll get it on now."

'Stephen replied, "It's gone too far now, he's not going to come."

'I said, "That's because he cannot come and have a proper fight, he's a proper mug."

'He couldn't run a nursery, he's a proper puke, he goes to places he can handle, that's all.'

Terry Mitchell takes up the story: 'Armstrong was on remand for demanding money on Newcastle's Gosforth High Street and he come in through the prison reception. We had the kids squared in reception and they told us everything, and he started squealing because he knew he'd have to come on B Wing with us, where we were all remanded. The busies, the CID, took him back out of Durham Prison and back to the police station and when he come back he said he'd be out in 28 days.'

Stu Watson: 'He come back on remand and Stephen and Michael Sayers were in and Nigel Abadom was in. Armstrong went to see Abadom and asked him to sort it out for him so he could come on to the yard at exercise time. He wouldn't come out on the yard because I was there.

'I was shouting up at his cell all the time, "Get on the yard then, Armstrong. Get on the yard and get it sorted out!"

'He wouldn't come on to the exercise yard at all and he wouldn't even go in the showers. He stayed up on the fours [fourth-floor landing] and he would not come out the cell when we were on exercise or on a visit. If Armstrong was on a visit the same time as us, they [prison officers] had to ask me not to do anything while in the visits room, saying they'd put him at the top end. Coincidentally, Vaughany [Stephen Vaughan] was visiting someone and they were up at the top end and I got restrained on the visit because I was going to do Vaughany.

'I knew I was in there as a direct result because he [Armstrong] wouldn't have a fight with me and he got Paul Ashton involved and that's when it all escalated to the gunfight we had with Ashton. One of the charges we were acquitted of was supposedly shooting Ashton on the Redheugh Bridge, which we were charged with at the same time as we were charged with the Malting House pub incident, which, according to Ashton's claims, happened in 1991.'

14

HOOD WITH A HEART

When it comes to having a soft heart, Viv was up there with the best. And, when it comes to hearing at first hand about this, we should listen to what John Davison has to say: 'I first started boxing as an amateur when I was 25. I had nothing else to do, I had just got married, I was living in a flat at Throckley in Newcastle and I had bought an MFI unit, an empty unit. I had nothing to put in it.

'A couple of lads invited, "Come to the gym in the West End."

'The coach there was Phil Fowler.

'I said, "It's a mug's game!"

'They persisted and said, "Come down, come down."

'So I went down and started punching the bag and Phil Fowler said, "Who do you box for?"

'I told him I hadn't boxed and he said, "You have!"

'I replied, "No, I haven't."

'I did some sparring with the lads and knocked three of them out. They just went crazy and I was told I should be a boxer. Again, I said it was a mug's game. Then again, I had this empty MFI unit with nothing to fill it, so I thought, I might as well box just to get a few trophies for the unit.

'After the first year I fought the world-ranked number one, a boxer called Paul Hodgkinson, an amateur, a great lad. In my first nine fights I had nine knockouts! They stuck me in the ABAs, the national championship, at featherweight. I knocked out Paul Hodgkinson in the first round and then I went on to captain England 17 times all over the world.

'Then I was picked for the Olympics and I trained for two years. Politics started to come into it, though. I had already fought a boxer called Michael Delaney and I beat him twice, but they sent him to the Olympics instead of me. There is a long story behind that: they just thought I was too aggressive; I'm more of an aggressive style, more of a professional style. When you box for England, they like a tippy-tappy boxer, jab and move. They don't go a lot for aggression and mine was a very aggressive style, so they didn't go along with that; amateurs don't really like that.

'I travelled all over the world and boxed the world-ranked number one; the world number two and the world number three. I won a silver medal against the world number two, Yuri Alexandrov, from Russia, so I naturally thought I was going to the Olympics and I wouldn't have turned pro. I was never at home; every weekend I was always training at Crystal Palace [in London]. It creased the wife when I was overlooked for the Olympics and Delaney was chosen instead, a man I had beaten twice! Delaney got beaten in his first fight at the Olympics. He didn't really seem to try; his heart wasn't in it by the look of it. I thought, I'm not going to box amateur any more. Kevin, the national coach, kept phoning me up asking me to stay on as an amateur, but it didn't change my mind.

'How Viv come into it was that when I turned professional I was looking for a sponsor and I was looking all over and somebody mentioned Viv's name. I asked him if he knew anybody who would sponsor me. Viv offered to sponsor me to the tune of £1,000, which helped me get all my gym equipment and other items. I had a proper gumshield, gloves, boots, headguard and a gown. Our sparring friendship grew, Viv used to come into the gym and spar with me. He couldn't believe how strong I was for a featherweight.

'Viv must have been around 18 or 20 stone at the time and he could punch, really punch. His hand speed was very fast, he was tremendously fast for a big fellow. Your hand speed is a lot different from your body speed and it was a natural thing he was doing when he was boxing. You train all the time with your hands, that's how you get your hand speed, but your top-half speed you go with the flow. Hand speed doesn't mean the rest of your body is fast. [This clearly accounts for Viv's ability to be able to sort out two or three men in seconds.]

'Personally speaking, I thought Viv was a great kid, a real nice gentleman. I didn't know anything about his lifestyle. He helped me out, he started me off in boxing, him and Rob Armstrong; they were the ones that gave me the money.

'When Viv was an amateur boxer, he thought about going professional. When we were sparring, I said that with his size and strength he could probably beat half the professionals in the country at that time. I used to say to him, "You want to turn professional."

'I had Viv's name on my gown in the last fight I had when

he was alive, as a "thank you" for him giving me that £1,000. I had "John Davison, Sponsored by Viv Graham" put on my gown, but the cameras avoided that area and it was covered over. It was just a friendly sort of thing to do, as he gave me the money to get me started off. I suppose he started my career. It might have seemed that I was advertising thuggery, but it was simply returning the favour. The first gloves that I won the World International title with, I'm sure I gave Viv those gloves.

'I was boxing in a booth on the Town Moor in Newcastle for a while at the beginning of my boxing career. I still have the same mates and when I won my first major title I was car-booting on the following Sunday. People were walking past and they couldn't understand why I was selling junk at a car-boot sale. I said I'm not going to change just because I've won the title. People automatically thought that because I was the champion I should change my personality.

'At the end of the day, your friends are more important than anybody else; you stick with the ones who you know. Some that are trying to be your friend are going behind your back calling you names; they're not your mates. So I've never changed, I've still got the same mates I had years ago and I still drink with the same mates.

'I remember when I was boxing in Manchester as a professional, I stopped my opponent and this little kid come up to me and he said, "I'm going to be a champion one day."

'I patted him on the head and said, "Good lad."

'It was the first time I met Naseem Hamed! We met years later in the Metro Centre [in Gateshead] when he made it big and he was fighting up here.

'I went along to see him and I said, "Can you remember?"

'He said, "Yes, I remember. Come on, let's have our photograph taken together."

'He's a good kid. The reason he isn't liked on television is because of the way he acts. It's all hype and that's what it's all about now. In real life, he's not that person as appears on the television.

'I have an interest in training people who want to box. Boxing training is the best fitness training in the world. Nobody has ever done what I have from Newcastle. The last man that won the British title from Newcastle was called Thomas Watson, 60 years ago. It was a job to me and that's it.

'I still do what I did all those years ago, antiques, car-boot sales, shopping and wheeling and dealing. When I was brought up, there were tin baths and outside toilets and that wasn't that long ago. Viv and I were brought together with a common bond and his background was not of any concern to me; we came together as sparring partners and that was my life at that time.

'My neighbours accept me as normal and no different to anyone else and that is the way I like it, although people do still come and shake my hand because it was only a few years ago that I retired.

'Amateur boxing now seems a waste of time because, if you get a head shot now, you get a standing count; it's so strict now because of the dangers involved. As for women boxers, I trained Audrey Godfrey, who was the first woman ever to fight in the ring up here. That is another piece of history I made. I do train quite a few women who do it for keep-fit purposes. It's great if you want extra stamina, to keep fit or you want to lose weight. Athletes should do more boxing training because it's the best training.

I help women who want to lose weight and feel good about themselves.

'Fifteen years ago, when it all started, I was pleased of Viv's help. I was pleased to present his kids with my gown so that his kids could say, "My dad sponsored John Davison, the first man in 60 years from Newcastle to win two World International titles and a British title."

'Thanks, Viv.'

15

YOU KNOW WHAT
MAKES A MAN TICK BY
HOW HE UNWINDS

Viv's fiancè, Anna Connelly, might be thought to have
been privy to all Viv's little secrets – but she wasn't!
Viv was a complex man with complex problems. He was
searching for something inside himself but was never to find
the key to life's problems.

At the time Anna first met Viv, he was unknown on
Tyneside. She takes up the story: 'When I met him in 1986,
he didn't have a name and at that time I was still married,
but separated. I was out on the town in Newcastle with my
sisters and the first thing I noticed about Viv were his
lovely teeth.

'I knew he was a nice person, but I didn't know who he
was. The very first time we met, he came across and asked
if he could buy me a drink; he bought us vodkas and we
were laughing together. We went back the next night and got
more vodka. We kept going for a few weeks, getting drinks

off him, and then Viv asked me out. My sister-in-law was in the town and one of Viv's friends said to her that I was seeing Viv Graham. I hadn't been seeing Viv at all up to this time because I was married, but my relationship wasn't very good. My sister-in-law went and told my husband that I was seeing Viv, we had a fight and after about five weeks we split up and I went to stay at my mam's.

'About three weeks after that, Viv found out and he came to see me and said, "You're not seeing your husband now, so will you go out with me on your own without your family?"

'Viv was a gentleman in every way, pulling seats out and opening doors. He was like that with everyone. Someone who was being nice to me made the difference, as I was not used to that.

'I remember Viv walking towards me with a big smile on his face and he said, "Do you ladies want a drink?"

'There was about six of us sitting there. He kept looking over all of the time, so I knew he wasn't going to come over and just ask the time. I wasn't aware that Viv was having a relationship with anyone else at that time. Although he said he had a few ex-girlfriends with kids to him and that he would always see his kids, he was a single, free man.

'At that time he had a daughter, Jodie Annie, to Julie Rutherford and had one son, Dean, to Gillian Lowes. I had been in love before, but not in this way. I'll probably not meet anyone again.

'Viv was still close to his children, Viv's parents love their grandchildren and were visited every day by them and Viv called to see them every day. Our relationship didn't interfere with this. It wasn't like a duty for him. He loved his kids. He loved to see them happy. He travelled to see them every day no matter what. At one time Viv started work as a labourer for John Wilkinson and he started travelling up to see his children at night-time so he could fit the job in. Viv was working on roofs and that helped supplement his income at that time.

'In the beginning he wasn't really known; the only thing he did was to have a few fights. His name wasn't big then, but as time went on it became bigger. He wasn't a villain; all what he used to do was have a fight. If you were in the pub and you were a big lad and were being cheeky and the manager said, "This man is being cheeky here," then Viv would come across and say, "Look, will you please leave the bar and stop causing trouble."

'He didn't come across and cause you trouble or beat you up. He would ask you a few times and if you didn't leave he would then hit you and knock you out. He didn't like picking things up and hitting you with it. When he hit them, he used to catch them before they fell and take them outside and wait with them until they came around and sent them on their way by saying, "Son, don't come back. I've asked you three times and then you wouldn't leave," and that was Viv.

'He wasn't a rotter like the West End lot, hitting you with anything, punching you all over and then kicking you down the stairs! Viv wouldn't dream of anything like that. People came for him to sort out the bother; he never ever asked them. People came to the door to ask him to go and sort trouble out in the bars, saying that the police had sent them.

'I had a marvellous lifestyle. I bought dresses and things from Peaches and Cream [shop that used to be in Newcastle city centre selling clothes for the elite]. Viv would buy me dresses valued at £600 and £700. He would spend £1,000 on a dress and shoes to match. Whatever I liked, he would buy it for me and that pleased him. As long as it made me happy, then he was happy. He liked to give things, but he didn't like them if they were short dresses! He would buy them and then when he got home, if he didn't like them, he wouldn't speak to you because they would be too revealing and he would say, "Have you seen how short that dress is?"

'I would say, "What did you buy it for then? You made me try it on in the shop!"

'Then we would start arguing and then the dress would get ripped up and that was the end of that.

'My mam would say, "What have you paid all that money for?"

'Viv would reply, "Well, Irene, it's bad enough being in the town watching your own back without lads looking at your lass with short frocks on – it just makes matters worse!"

'I stormed to my mother, "He just wants me to wear polo necks and long skirts."

'I didn't want to wear them because I was only in my twenties.

'He underestimated himself all of the time and he was a bundle of nerves and his stomach used to turn over! He really underestimated himself and he'd end up sitting on the toilet. He was never "I'm Viv Graham, don't mess with me!" He was never like that; he didn't have loads of confidence. If he ever lost a bit of weight, he would think he was too small. He was never six foot-odd tall, yet his father was. Viv was only five foot eleven inches tall.

'He would be worried if he got involved in a fight with a gang! Viv never had loads of confidence and he loved to be really big and if he looked in the mirror and he was really big, then he was happy! He was big, but if he lost any weight he didn't like that and felt uncomfortable. It was because of his name really, but he never used to be that big when he boxed, as his weight was only 13 stone. He could do the same when he was big as he could do at 13 stone; he was actually fitter. Then he got into the body-building stuff and he went even bigger! He got involved because a lot of his friends were doing that and eating the tuna and chicken. When he was in the gym, it was one against the other; he didn't want to be fat, though.

'He went to the gym two or three times a day, and he did once try steroids by injection, but he took bad with them and he ended up with an abscess on his backside and he needed an operation [this was declared on his insurance application when he was asked about his health]. He was frightened of needles.

'I said, "I'm telling your dad on you."

'He used to get in bad tempers, but he never touched the kids or me. He used to pull the doors off, but I wasn't bothered because he used to replace them the next day. The confidence he lacked, the steroids gave him. He couldn't ever get the confidence because he wasn't an aggressive man. He couldn't get into a bad temper easy. It used to take him a long time to get like that. People used to worry, thinking he was getting softer. When he was supposed to do things he couldn't get the aggression there. But with steroids the aggression came straight away, but then that wasn't him. He knew where the aggression was coming from [steroids] and he decided himself to come off them because his dad said, "You don't need steroids, son. You're a big lad."

'Viv was disciplined because of the boxing he started when he was 13. Boxing training was really well disciplined and he did that right up until he was in his twenties. Most people that ever met him knew that he was a gentleman and very soft-hearted. He could easily cry over his nanna's memories. He always had a wreath at Christmas to put on her grave.

'Viv used to give me chocolates and flowers as a romantic gift, but he never wrote me any poetry as he wasn't a good writer ... but he could write a bet out, no problem.

'He used to nip into town and get me make-up and lipstick and buy me nice underwear. He went into that shop called Secrets, regardless of his size and being well known. It never bothered him a little bit and if I ran out of a lipstick then I would say, "Oh! My make-up!"

'He'd say, "Where's it from?"

"Fenwicks!" I replied.

'Straight away, he'd run there.

'If I wanted stockings, he'd ask, "What colour do you want?"

'If I wanted lipsticks, he got me ten lipsticks. Viv and his friend Alan Rooney, who was with him every single day, went for the make-up.

'Alan was later charged with blackmail because of something he got involved with and it was traced back to Alan because his child had picked the telephone up and said, "Hello?" That's how he got caught in a blackmail plot when he had threatened a publican's husband with Viv, because the man had used Viv's name in vain. This other man was using Viv's name, but Alan ended up getting eight years for something stupid like that. [In Alan Rooney's case, it would seem that the word 'blackmail' should be changed to 'demanding money with menaces'. If you play with fire, you get burned. This publican wanted the best of both worlds: he wanted to use the threat of Viv without any expense being involved. Rooney was simply capitalising on that.]

'Alan was just out of hospital after that, having had some sort of virus; he was really bad with it! It took over his whole body and, you know when you see someone with multiple sclerosis, he was just like that for months and months.

'Alan was at our house every day, but Viv had been told when he was in the town that this man [the one Rooney eventually blackmailed] had been using Viv's name. Alan had no money and said, "Should I phone him up and say whatever?"

'Viv said, "Do what you want."

'I think he [Rooney] said, "I'll burn your house down."

'But he had no intentions of doing it. That man was in the wrong, he knew he had used Viv's name and was taking money off people. He really thought Viv was going to get him because he had done wrong.

'Before Alan had done all this, Viv and I had went to that man once and he had given Viv money for something he had done. From then on, he thought he was well in with Viv, sort of thing: "I've give Viv a bit job and paid him some money, me and Viv are like that."

'That's when he started using Viv's name and getting a lot of money out of it for himself. Viv never knew nothing about it, he never seen that man again. The publican was from over the water, Sunderland. He had a pub in Hylton or some place like that.

'Alan got eight years for that when really that man was in the wrong. It never happened that way; it just so happened Viv died and then the man wouldn't drop the charges, but if Viv had still been alive he wouldn't have had Alan charged because he knew the publican was in the wrong.

'Even if the man hadn't paid Alan, Alan wasn't really bothered, he was just testing him. It was a stupid thing. It ended up Viv died and obviously he couldn't go to court on Alan's behalf, but, had he been alive, he would have went to court as a witness. By this time Alan knew who the man had been taking money off by using Viv's name.

'When Viv lost his driving licence for 12 months, Alan was the one to drive him around. That was another story. Viv went to pick the kids up and this woman stepped straight off the kerb and he bumped into her; luckily she wasn't hurt. I went straight to the scene and found her with broken glasses. A couple living opposite had seen it happen and phoned me up and I went straight there. Viv was absolutely devastated!

'The woman said, "Son, I'm all right! I'm all right!"

'She had a pound coin in her hand; she was running for the bus.

Viv gave her £200 to replace the broken glasses; we went to the flower shop and got a big bouquet of flowers for her, found out where she lived and went back to the house with the flowers and gave her another £100. Her husband was there when this took place and she again said, "Son, I'm all right, I've just got a little bit of a headache where the glasses have caught me."

'Within six weeks she took a private summons out and got him done. As it happened, his car wasn't insured. She thought she would get a lot of money and then she claimed she was getting severe headaches, but, when she issued a private summons and the police wanted Viv's documents, he wasn't insured and he lost his licence. She still carried on with the private summons; someone must have told her who Viv was and that he had money. She couldn't do anything about it because Viv died before it reached court.

'Viv was genuinely sick with it. He gave her that money

and was worried about her regardless of the insurance, as he did not know his insurance had expired. The old lady said she was over the moon with the money, her glasses weren't even worth £200, but she still done that and took him to court. That will show you what type of a person Viv was.

'When people asked Viv to do them a favour, he always had respect for the elderly and many a time turned down a job if the person he had to go and see was old. Many a time, though, he didn't really have to do anything. A lot of businessmen came to him. Say, for instance, you had fitted windows to a house and you knew you weren't going to get the money, [you] would go to Viv for help to get it. Then the money would be there the next day when Viv called to collect it.

'Some of the things said about Viv were all lies, saying things like he was a big drug baron! He never ever dealt in drugs! That was one thing he never ever touched! He never needed to deal in drugs; he made a lot of money from other things. He had bars and nightclubs from Whitley Bay through to Wallsend and Shields Road into the town [Newcastle city centre].

'Some weeks he picked up maybe £15,000, which was apart from businessmen and other people knocking at the door. I was there when Viv had to collect £60,000 and he got £30,000 in a carrier bag; he never needed to touch drugs. People just accepted what was put out about him. No one would stand up and defend him when he passed away.

'Viv never thought of what he could do with his money. He did at the finish with this house, but before that he wasn't interested, he just liked to spend it; he didn't drink and he didn't smoke … he just liked a bet. Viv could have bought the house outright, he could have bought his car outright, but he got it all on finance. After Viv's death, his dad paid for his car every week.

'He liked it better that way, getting the house on a mortgage. He didn't have a penny put to one side for emergencies! As quick as it came in, the quicker it went out. He could have had £30,000 in that hand and within an hour he wouldn't have £1 for the electric meter! It never bothered him; he knew if he spent it by the Monday he would have more by the weekend. Tomorrow didn't matter, he lived for the day and I was just the same.

'At times it was a competition to see who could win the most money. Every day we were in the bookies', he would say, "There's your money."

'I would put a bet on and say, "Give me £100 so I can put this bet on."

'I would maybe win because I was luckier than he was.

'I still put the odd bet on now. I had done that prior to meeting Viv. We bought a greyhound and it cost us a fortune; it didn't come anywhere in the races it ran in, but we could watch it in the races and have a night out. We even thought about buying a racehorse, but that's as far as it went.

'We had 32 rabbits, two geese, five dogs and 36 chickens and they took a lot of looking after. Viv loved the chickens and collecting the eggs in the morning. Although Viv ate chicken for his meals when he trained, he wouldn't have been able to eat one of these chickens for Sunday dinner. He went shooting with his dad, but he couldn't have shot anything we had just for the sake of eating it. He shot at pheasants in the wild on these shoots, but that was it.

'Viv and I didn't lead a boring life; we went to the best of restaurants and everything. Viv didn't like paying his debts, although he did pay up in the end. If we got anything on HP, it would end up not getting paid, so we used to buy things outright. A television man knocked on the door and Viv wouldn't pay him. When he seen it was Viv he didn't come back.

'The poll-tax man came and he saw Viv and asked who he was and I just said something like, "He's my brother." We were all laughing.

'Viv said, "You'll get no money from here!"

'The man said, "I'm away, me." He didn't come back.

'He loved life and he was up at six o'clock in the morning with the dogs. He was even happier when we got Buster [a dog]. There was a big field at the back and he was looking forward to getting up and running because he loved training. He used to make me get up with him and wanted me to run around the field with him! I still had my pyjamas on and used to walk around the field with the dogs. The neighbour next door used to laugh when he seen me out with him.

'Viv didn't like me smoking because he didn't, so he limited me to ten cigarettes a day, but I had my secret supply hidden. I used to keep the same packet and top it up.

'He would say, "You've only had two tabs today!"

'Although Viv went into an environment where there was cigarette smoke, he didn't like me smoking because it was bad for my health. He couldn't stand the smell of the smoke and he used to get bathed and showered two or three times a day. Every time he came back from the gym or from somewhere smelly, he would have a shower. We had someone come in and help out with the cleaning so we didn't have a big pile of ironing building up in the corner.

'As for Viv's safety, he confided in me about this and many a time raised his concerns about him or I being shot.

'He used to say all the time, "I'll never reach 40 because, I'm telling you, they'll shoot me."

'I thought he was invincible and nothing could happen to him. I just thought that when he said it that they would be too frightened to come and they wouldn't try it.

'A gang of masked men came to my house when I lived in Daisy Hill at Wallsend and the windows come in! There were two carloads of them and they had masks on and were carrying guns! Viv didn't hide from anyone and his telephone number was available from the telephone directory.

'We used to go on holiday and our favourite place was Greece. I would see a different Viv. We never ever went where it was lively; sometimes we were the only people on the beach. We would come back, get changed and go for a meal. We didn't ever go to Tenerife, though, as it was reported that Viv had been there and had a fight with a man called Andy Winder. Winder did timeshare in Tenerife. [Winder was originally from Darlington and it was alleged that he placed a £30,000 hit on Viv that was to be carried out should anything happen to him. The reason for this allegation was, it was claimed, that Winder had come off worse in a fight between the pair. However, that fight did not take place, so this story is unfounded and will always remain just that: a story.]

'Paddy wanted Viv to come across and do the timeshare. Viv had discussed this with his dad as he always did and his dad said, "No way!"

'There are things coming out these last few years that even I didn't know about because I was so high on Valium! In all of that time there are things I am just starting to question now.

'When we went on holiday we went there as a family and we didn't want to come back. We wanted it to last for ever and wanted to move away, but we said we'd just stay here for a few years. He loved the country and he wanted to be away, but his work was here and he was becoming more established. Half the time he didn't even have to show his face; he had the likes of Rob Armstrong and them in nightclubs overseeing it for him.

'Viv was going to get contracts on the books and do it properly; some jobs could pay £1,000 a week. That was just happening before he died. It was all coming together, he was going to give the town up and leave it at that. He was sick of having to put his face up against it all of the time. People wanted to use Viv's name above their doors.

'I remember Higgins Security, they came from Birmingham and asked Viv to visit them there and meet their top bosses. Viv told his dad and he was told not to go there and to make them come here to meet him. They told Viv they didn't want to take over the town because they knew he was Viv Graham.

'A lot of the doormen were complaining because they feared Higgins were coming here to Newcastle and taking their jobs and they were saying to Viv, "You'll have to stop them because they're taking our jobs! You'll have to show them!"

'They knew all about Viv and he went to see them and they said they had no intentions of taking over the bars. Viv sorted that entire lot out for them.'

Returning to Viv's more private side, Anna said, 'Viv hated me wearing short skirts and sometimes he went overboard. I remember once when we were out, off he went to the toilet through a crowd of women and he would keep his hands in the air. If he seen anyone touch a woman and they complained, he didn't take kindly to that happening, especially if it was to me.

'I remember once when someone was talking to me, Viv went across and said, "That was my wife!" They didn't do it again.

'When I first met Viv, he was with me constantly, but sometimes there would be one night when he wouldn't be there and the next day I would say, "Where were you?"

'He would tell me a pack of lies and say, "Oh, I was in the casino in the town until seven o'clock this morning. I had my breakfast."

'Which was a load of crap! Viv's best quality was his kindness; if he had a fault, then it was being overly generous. People would call, crying, to the door, saying they had a gas bill. He would pull the money out and give it to them, but he never got it back from them.

'I don't think Viv was trying to overcompensate because he was a non-believer. I was a good Catholic. Viv's funeral was in a Protestant church, although he wasn't a believer in God and had no intention of accepting my faith, so he had no reason to want to prove something. I believe he started to believe in God more, although his father was a staunch non-believer. I think it was because Viv got on well with Father Conaty and the fact that when missionaries from Bosnia started coming to our house we put them up. It was through me that he started to change his views.

'I remember it was the first Holy Communion of one of my daughters and the table was full of religious gifts; Viv bought the full whack for all the kids there. Once you met him, you never forgot him and I used to say to the Father that he was something special because he was somebody special to me. I couldn't believe how very kind in his ways he was and yet still had this power inside him. He was very strong, he could lift a 580-pound bench-press, not a problem to him. He gave a lot of help to the local boxing club and had the heating put in and did a lot more; Viv paid for everything.

'We had our arguments, just like anybody else. Viv would come back from the gym, lie on the settee, have loads of sweets and watch videos. That's what he liked the most; he would lock the door and take the phone off the hook.

'As for children, I didn't think we needed a child to cement our relationship and Viv didn't because I had my children and he had his children, but then there came a point when he did. We did try, but it just never happened. I went to the doctor and put a pregnancy test in and I was frightened to say the real results after the way Viv went on. We came out of the surgery and I told him I was pregnant and he jumped for joy and wanted to tell everyone. We rushed back home and he was starting to telephone his mother!

'I put the receiver down and said, "I've got something to tell you."

'I was frightened after the way he went on. I thought, Eh! Why did I say that to him?

'I said, "I was only pretending."

'He went, "You *what*?"

'I said, "I just pretended to you just to see what you would think."

'He was gutted, really gutted, and then I realised he really did want a baby. I was frightened in case I had one, as he wouldn't love my kids in the same way. We did want one then – this was about three months before he died – so we did start and try. He loved them and they loved him and they even called him their dad. He spent more time with them than he did with his own kids.

'I was from a mixed family and I knew there might be problems, as I had some problems in my family, although they weren't problems of a bad nature. Because I had the experience from that, I thought that Viv might encounter some problems with that scenario.

'Viv said, "I would treat them exactly the same."

'I said, "Other people's are never the same as your own. Your two come here and I love them, but I don't love them as I love my own."

'So I knew, if I had ever had a baby, then that love would have been a special love, different to the love he would have for them. This would have caused arguments and I didn't want that because we had a happy relationship. I didn't want that. I didn't want to start fighting. I knew he really did want a baby and we did try.

'My children said, "We can have a little baby sister or a baby brother."

'They [Anna's two daughters, Dominique and Georgia] talk about him every day. They've got their pictures [of him] in their rooms and they talk about him all the time. They absolutely loved him. She's [Dominique] got her own little book that she makes her own little poems in. The kids put the monkey hanging on the rear-view mirror that was in Viv's car and he just left it there.

'Sometimes Viv's business and private life overlapped. He would call me and come and get something to eat, then he would go straight back out to the gym and from there on to the bookies. He would come out, go for something to eat and go and get some videos, then, seven o'clock, he would ask us if we wanted anything from the shop. He would watch a video with his bag of sweets, with the phone off the hook and the door locked. If something cropped up, which usually it did, he would take me with him and I would sit in the car waiting. My sister, Mary, and him were very close; she would stand up to anybody, even a man!

'Just after I had lost Viv, there was further tragedy when my brother-in-law, Harry Thompson, was tragically lost to violence. Mary's husband had gone to sort out someone who had burgled his home and he was stabbed. I couldn't believe it. He died about nine months after Viv. I was just starting to get back on my feet. I couldn't believe it; I just couldn't believe it.

'Viv's teeth were his pride and joy. Viv was going to have gold fillings in some of them; he liked to look after his teeth. A ship had pulled into the Tyne and the sailors were causing bother. One of them was a championship boxer about six foot ten tall. He touched a woman's behind.

'Viv said, "Here, you wouldn't do that where you come from, so you won't do that here in Newcastle, touching lasses' backsides."

'So he [the sailor] takes his sunglasses off and said, "Who are you, man?"

'Viv said, "Never mind who I am!"

He [the sailor] just went bop! Viv's tooth went through his lip. Anyway, Viv banjoes him and the sailor went down. The police were sitting in their car watching it. They said they seen the big black man and stood up for Viv, as a lot of the police liked Viv. Viv got away with that one.

'Where we used to live was terrible! There was smack and heroin! You could go and knock on any door and get it. When the football club was there, Viv would take about

50 kids on the field and he would say, "Don't take drugs, get training."

'Kids loved him; if they could get into the car with him it made their day. I knew all the hard men you could think of or name and Viv was nothing like that. If Viv hit you, he wouldn't let you fall in case you hit your head on the ground. Viv never took liberties with people, yet they did and they are all still alive. Viv first started in Wheelers nightclub and he had trouble with a Gateshead man called Paul Ashton, now serving 31 years for violence!

'Viv wouldn't use his power against someone weighing only about eight or nine stones; he would pull his punch back. Viv gave Stevie the Hammer a nasty bash! I was there when it happened. I didn't like fighting and it wasn't as if it was a fight that would last for ages. Viv was as fast as lightning!

'If you were a big person, he knew how to punch through the boxing, so if you were a big person he would give a harder punch. He wouldn't punch a man of eight stones the way he punched Stevie the Hammer because it would have punched their face in. After all of that, Stevie did not hold any grudge against Viv. He thought the world of Viv and they still remained friends even though that happened, and Viv thought a lot of Stevie.

'Every night I go to bed and I can't sleep very well. I might sleep maybe about two and a half to three hours. I must be in a deep sleep because by the next day I'm fit enough and not worn out. I'm always on the go, so that must be all I need. Before Viv died, you couldn't get me out of bed. I could sleep and sleep and sleep.

'Viv's views on someone who committed crimes against old people were what you would expect from someone like him. Viv had no proper friends except for those in my family, who were really close to him. Since he died, I can say he has no friends. No one has given me any support that could be looked at as anything real.

'Mind you, Rob Bell has helped; they were very good to Viv's family, but the rest of them just used him.

'It was said that Viv was put into prison for a savage attack on Stuart Watson. Why didn't they say that the man Viv attacked was 18 ½ stone? Eventually Viv and Stuart became friends because after Viv got out of prison things were said and the air needed clearing, so Viv went to see Stuart and the matter was settled without the use of violence. Viv was invited to parties that Stuart held, so that proves Viv wasn't a thug, as some portrayed him.

'Viv's boxing career led to an involvement with a fellow heavyweight amateur boxer, Manny Burgo, from South Shields. The boxing selectors choose Manny over and above Viv to go and box for the championships. Viv wasn't very happy at this and Manny said, "Viv, it wasn't my fault."

'This is what made Viv throw the towel in, as he knew he was a better boxer than Manny, but Manny was chosen because he looked a better boxer. People say it was because of a frozen shoulder that Viv stopped, but that was the real reason. He went back to boxing after that, though, for a while.

'I remember the Tim Healy carry-on. Viv didn't need to live up to people; he liked to be on his own. We were out in Julie's nightclub one night when Viv was involved in a fight and there were loads of them. Viv was fighting with these men and everybody that knew Viv had moved away from him over to the other side, but Tim Healy hadn't! He come up to Viv to pass by and was clipped, but Viv hadn't

realised it was Tim Healy and it wasn't until afterwards that
they said, "You've hit Tim Healy!" Viv thought that he was
going to get the police involved. There was a joke that Pat
Roach would be coming in to get Viv. Roach was a real-life
professional wrestler who played a part in *Auf
Wiedersehen, Pet*.

'Viv's hero was his dad and his favourite film was *Zulu*.
There was only one man Viv looked up to and that was his
dad. I feel that I could help anyone that ever suffered the
loss of a loved one. After the loss of Harry, my brother-in-
law, I became stronger again.

'Viv was a real professional, he looked after you, but, as
for himself, he only lived for the day. He didn't put
anything to one side for a rainy day. If he got older and
couldn't do that profession any more, then he might have
thought about it.

'We did once try to save; we opened a bank account for a
mortgage. He gave me £200 to put into the bank and I asked
for a balance, which was given to me as £2.82.

'I said, "You had better check it, as that's not right!"

'The clerk said, "Well, how much?"

'I replied, "There's a lot of money in, you'd better
check it."

'So she checked it all and said, "There's definitely only
£2.82 left in the account."

'I said, "Well, you'd better get the manager because
there's definitely more. I know what I put in!"

'When all came to all, Viv had been going in and signing
a piece of paper and getting the money out for the bookies.

'Another woman come and said, "Your Viv's been
coming in and signing the piece of paper and drawing out
every week."

'I wasn't bothered, I went back to the bookies and pulled him; he was full of himself, laughing! He knew when I went in what he had done.

'I said, "You're joking, there's me going in and them saying there's only £2.82. Well, that's me finished."

'So I let that one go and I never ever tried to save again. The bank book is still upstairs with £2.82 in.

'My brother, my sister and her husband loaned me the £12,000 as a deposit on this house. We didn't ever get to pay the mortgage, as Viv died. There was an insurance policy that covered it, but it wasn't paid out because it was in probate because Gillian Lowes is contesting it.' [Since this interview the insurance payout has been settled and all have received some sort of payment.]

'People knew what Viv was capable of and he didn't use a weapon. They knew he would come face to face with them and what they didn't know was that he would always give them a chance. He wouldn't just run, he would say to them, "Look don't do that, don't be like ..." and if he got another phone call about them, then they were in bother, but he would let them walk away. That's why they kept coming back, because they knew really at the bottom of him he was ... She [Anna nods in her mother's direction] knew him to knock a kid out and then give him money after he'd done it.

'One Saturday afternoon we were going for a meal and we bumped into a man Viv knew; he was called Durant. We were out on a Saturday afternoon shopping and going for a meal when Durant stopped us and took his coat off and said to Viv, "I can't work anywhere; you stopped me from working. I've got a mortgage!"

'Viv said, "Me? Not me! I wouldn't stop you working anywhere."

'Durant then said, "I've had enough."'

'Viv said to the man's wife, "Tell your man to put his coat back on."'

'Viv was on parole; he'd just got out of jail and he didn't want to have a fight and he wouldn't. They had a scuffle; the lad fell off the kerb and Viv picked him up and gave him £50 and said, "I'll give you a job any time."'

'It was Rob Armstrong whom Durant had a [fist] fight with, not Viv, but the rumour was Viv wouldn't let Durant work on any of the doors in the town. A fight happened between Durant and Rob Armstrong some time, months earlier, in Madison's nightclub and it had resulted in some damage to this man's eye. Viv was being blamed for it, but it wasn't him who did it.

'I know by when he died that people who I never knew wrote to me saying that they felt safe when Viv was around and that people felt safe when Viv was watching the bars and clubs. Some of the TV documentaries shown made Viv seem like that doorman who glassed that woman in Manchester. That was horrible, it made people think Viv was like that.

'The stories about Viv weren't balanced, especially when it showed Viv setting about that club doorman. The reason for the attack was that this man had allegedly attacked two ten-stone lads and smashed their jaws, as far as I was told when we came back off holiday. [Author's note: Stuart Watson was assaulted in a totally unprovoked attack instigated by people who wanted to oust him from his job of stopping them entering certain nightspots in Newcastle.]

'At the same time the Sayers gang went to Hobo's and, as far as I knew, they had a falling-out with Stuart Watson. They come up to Viv because at that time they were friendly with Viv and they said that the doorman wouldn't let them in there. "Come down with us, Viv?"

'Viv didn't have a clue that Watson was in there [Hobo's] or that it was Stuart Watson on the door. Viv had been looking for Watson, as the manager had been in and said that Watson had been in and broke one of their jaws and that was the message Viv had been given from the manager of a nightclub.

'Viv was portrayed as being a horrible man savaging that man. You tell the story, though, of a man who was 18 ½ stone and little men who were only 10 stone and that tells a different story to the one reported on TV and in the press. Viv was standing up for the little man, but in doing so he was made out to be the bully, which was not so.

'Viv and the Sayers fell out when he was in jail and they didn't make it up. He also fell out with Rob Armstrong, but they made it up, although they weren't as close.

'Finally, I would like to say that, contrary to a well-known villain saying that Viv was supposed to be a grass, Viv was never a grass and, if he was, why won't they stand up? It's easy to say these things, because he's not here! Why can't they stand up and say their name if they say he was a grass and tell me what his name is and get the police to come forward to say what Viv was supposed to have grassed to them about?'

A poem written by Anna's daughter Dominique is dedicated to Viv, whom she calls 'Dad'.

To My Dad, Viv

What is goodbye? Just a word that makes us cry;
When a soul-like ship pulls from the shore.

VIV GRAHAM

In a place where I've been just last night in a dream;
Each saying, 'Don't cry for me for I am waiting for you.'

In this world of summer's blue the land of eternity;
When I asked, 'Can I stay?' they led me away saying,
'It's not your time; there are songs you must sing and
plant seeds in the spring.'

Lots of Love
Viv

Dominique

16

THE GRASSHOPPER
AND THE SQUIRREL

Who would know the real Viv Graham better than his parents, Eric and Hazel? Eric prefers to be called Jack and from now on that is how he will be referred to.

Jack and Hazel got to see their little Viv – the middle child of three; Karen was his younger sister and Eric his older brother – become big Viv. He made them proud, not just because of the boxing medals and cups he won or the football talent he possessed as a schoolboy, but because of his kind and gentle nature.

The first thing you notice about Jack Graham are his deep, dark and powerful eyes, and the determination in them. The light caught his shaven head and then I noticed that his hands were as large as shovels; the one that met mine seemed to be twice as big as my own size-11 hand.

Jack talked about the Hobo's nightclub incident, as a result of which Viv was convicted of a vicious unprovoked assault: 'Our Viv was at the court case, there was Stephen Sayers, Davie Lancaster, [Alan] "Fish" Tams and there was a sixth lad and they were looking for him. He was going into Durham Jail every week visiting them. I don't know if somebody must have tumbled, but it was weeks after, because they chased him, busies in their cars, and they caught him outside Durham.

'The busies had got the lot and fetched it in as an affray. If you seen the tape, from them going through the door to them coming out, it was only minutes. Three minutes, it took three minutes. Now then, there were two busies in Hobo's and they were on surveillance for drugs. They were from Tadcaster, they were Yorkshire busies; they weren't from here.

'The policeman said he had never seen a fight like it in his ten years on the police force. He said that our Viv started on Stuey Watson, moved off, two attacked him, kicking and punching, they come off and the other three went in kicking and punching.

'So that's six blokes kicking and punching one man and, if you look at the video, Stuey Watson comes out and he's hardly got a mark on him. How they can tell me ... I mean, six old pensioners should have put him in hospital. You've got six blokes kicking hell out of him. They said to the busy, "Why didn't you show your warrant card?"

'They said, "We were on surveillance."

'They were asked, "What would happen if a lass was getting raped, would you have just sat back and watched it, like?"'

What about Viv's friends, could they have helped out? Jack replied to this question with a certain amount of anger in his voice that sums up his feelings about those who were supposedly his son's friends. 'I'll tell you, and you can put this in the bloody book as well, they weren't friends, they were hangers-on; he was a money box for them.'

Jack continued in the same vein, saying, with sadness in his voice, 'And he was a minder for them! That's what he was.' Jack was speaking for a lot of people when he added, 'When they were with Viv Graham, they were ten foot tall! "Oh, I know Viv Graham, good friend of mine," so people would back off.'

He related an incident in which his son exercised his right as a private citizen to carry out some late-night security work. 'At the top end of the village, a lot of old people live and they were forever getting robbed. So he went up and sat in an old woman's house all night, sat in the chair all night, waiting, and nothing turned up.

'So he went to a certain party and said, "Look, if another one of those houses gets done I'm coming for you. Even if you haven't done it, I'm coming for you; I'm going to make a job of you, so spread the word, you're the one that's going to get it."

'It stopped. Christmas, before he died, when he was shopping with Anna and an old lady wanted a turkey, he said to Anna, "Keep her occupied."

'He went into a butcher's shop and came back and said, "There you are, mother, there's your Christmas dinner."

'They don't know about them things and when he sponsored the footballers and the boxing, things like that. He gave a kid [young father Pip Wright] £500 the week before Christmas: he hadn't a penny, he couldn't get the kids anything for Christmas.

'Viv said, "There's no kid should get up on Christmas morning without presents, give me it back when you've got it." That's the way Viv was.'

Viv's mother, Hazel, has endured poor health but she's a strong-willed lady. She said of her son: 'He saved Rob Bell's life.'

'If Rob knew that we were here, he would …' Jack put in, then just as quickly moved on to another matter: 'Our Viv bumped into him [Peter Donnelly] in the fish bar in the Green Market, he was crying to our Viv saying, "Divent hit me."

'Viv said, "I'm not going to hit you, don't worry."

'You see, the trouble is –' Jack took a breath as if it was releasing a great burden from him to be able to say this to someone, maybe for the first time '– he couldn't be a bloody gangster at all, he was too soft. You get these that lend you money and if you don't pay it, it's doubled and then a good thumping and then you get a leg broken the next time. He was too soft.

'Mind, when he kicked off, if he had a fight, he could go, there's nobody ever done it yet …' Jack reminded himself of his son's absence when he continued, 'well, they'll never do it now. He was hard, that way it was good, but the other way; he was as soft as claggy taffy [sticky toffee]. He was as easy for a hard-luck story …'

'He could cry like any other man,' Hazel added.

'He was as soft as clarts that way,' Jack went on.

Jack talked of Inspector Peter Durham, saying, 'He tried all ways to get our Viv. [Superintendent Peter Durham said in January 1994, after Viv's death, 'There is only one law-enforcement agency on Tyneside … Northumbria Police.'] When Viv came out of prison, they were following him in the car and taking photographs of him. They went around the town [Newcastle] and followed him all over and he just used to go, "All right, lads."

'The surprising thing is, what a hell of a lot got on with

him. From what I've heard, all the jumpy jacks are back in the town on the happy baccy and the stuff now, and people won't go back into the town. People are just petrified, where at one time you could go and sit and have a good night out with nothing to worry about.'

Hazel gave her account of meeting one of the Sayers family: 'I met Stephen Sayers when our young Viv [Viv's son] was poorly in hospital; he was a gentleman. I couldn't get over him; he was at the hospital at eight o'clock in the morning when I walked into the [Tyneside] General [Hospital].

'He said, "I'm sorry I've met you under these circumstances."'

'Viv was still in prison and they'd let him out, so he come to see little Viv.'

Jack clarified how Stephen Sayers was out of prison before his son: 'They got two years and our Viv got three. So they were out, but he was at the hospital to see the bairn. They were all friends then.'

After his prison sentence, Viv went his own way. Jack explained, 'Wor Viv was always a loner, though. I mean, if somebody said, "I'll fettle Viv Graham!" he would jump in the car and he would go to that place where this bloke had said what he was going to do. "Where's so and so? I'm here."

'"He's not in."'

'"Well, I'll be back tomorrow night."'

'Whereas now they take teams with them to back themselves up with! He didn't need that sort of backup. He would go in, and he'd never been to that place in his life and wouldn't know the bloke from Adam. He had no fear.'

Viv got on with people and, as an example, Jack mentioned the ex-pro boxer Manny Burgo. 'They had a fight [as amateurs] and Viv braed the living hell out of him, because his old man said to Viv, "You did that to my son."

'There were two of the judges sacked through that fight; they gave it to Manny Burgo because he was the English amateur champion. Viv never boxed for years and he was finished with the boxing, but he still had the fight with Manny. Viv had not fought for years; he won the Northern ABA championships in 1977, and he had three fights in the one night down at South Shields to win it. He then went to Denmark to fight. He was in Liverpool and he developed a frozen shoulder and got beat. He just concentrated on weight training and running, but you know what happens once you start hanging about with lasses: training's out the window.'

Jack mimicked a woman speaking, 'You think more of bloody football than you do of me.'

All around him laughed and he continued in his normal voice, 'You know what they are like. So he just pursued weight training.'

Hazel made an important point: 'He was never in trouble with the police as a teenager, never. He [Jack] used to say to Viv, "Burgle anybody or rob them and me and you are finished," you know.'

Jack confirmed this: 'I said, if you ever come in here and have been doing a house or drugs, that's me and you done.'

On the way Viv would seek advice from his father, Hazel says, 'He used to come here on a Sunday morning, after he'd been to the nightclub. We used to always have loads of company and he used to say to everybody, "Right, I want to talk to my father. Everybody out!"

'It didn't matter who was in,' Hazel continued. 'In fact, when this came out about Viv, I didn't even know anything existed.'

Here Jack helped her out. 'We didn't know half nor quarter of what went on, that was his business. He was a man for himself, you make your bed, you can lie in it. What you do is your business, but, as I say, drugging and anything dodgy like that, I don't agree with. I've never agreed with it. As I say, he's a man for himself and we don't know half nor quarter of what he did or didn't do down there [Newcastle].'

Jack was speaking with wisdom when he added, 'It's a different ball game doon the toon. They can buy you at one end of the street and sell you at the other end.'

What about when Viv wanted to relax? 'We used to go shooting at Haydon Bridge,' Jack said. 'Everything just seemed to lift off him. I don't know how you explain it, but it was like waking up on a Sunday morning.'

'He delivered a ferret,' Hazel recalled. 'He sent it by taxi with a note that read: "I love you, Dad. Here's a present for you." It was a live ferret! The poor man [the taxi driver].'

Jack explained how Viv came to send the ferret to him: 'There were some kids knocking a ferret around the street and he gave them £2. He said, "Here's £2, I'll buy that ferret off you."

'He then said to the taxi driver, "Here, take that, here's the address, give that to my father."

'The brother-in-law's got it. Viv sent it all the way from Wallsend.'

Jack added, 'There were lads with pigeon lofts out the back and, when he was young, he used to get squealers, little 'uns, off the lads. He had about a dozen or more. We used to put them in a cardboard box and put them in the wagon and get away over to Whitehaven and I would let them out. Viv would say that they had got back at such and such a time. They were just pets, eh, man!'

Jack talked of how he has an aversion to reporters and said, 'That fettled me with *The Cook Report* on television on the Thursday night, and on the Sunday morning I saw the headline "£2m Drug Baron".

'I said they are not worth a bottle of pop. And then *The Cook Report*: they tried to make wor Viv out as bad as them that done that manageress up in Manchester. I said it wouldn't have been as bad if that's what it was about, but it had nowt to do with security, protection, drugs, drinking – it was just a sham.'

The Cook Report documentary about club doormen is claimed to have caused trouble for the Graham household. Jack expressed his anger about this: 'If I had been a stranger and I had seen that on television, I would say, "He must be a wicked pig, him!"

'People that didn't know Viv would say he was nasty, but it had nothing to do with the programme, but the buggers stuck it in about protection. So when I seen *The Cook Report* and I knew that things were wrong within it, I then wondered how many more *Cook Reports* are wrong and have been twisted to make them look worse than what they are?

'If I was walking along the Quayside and a little bairn fell in the Tyne and I dived in and got it out, there would be little mention about that. But, if I walked down the Quayside and picked a kid up and threw him in the river, there would be headlines this big,' said Jack, holding his hands wide apart.

Jack was asked about Viv's apprenticeship days as a doorman, under the watchful eye of Gateshead's Billy Robinson, and he said, 'He was as green as grass when he started at the Hedgefield.'

Hazel disputed this, saying, 'It was in Burnopfield, the Travellers' Rest.'

But Jack continued, 'He started working in a number of pubs, as the person owned three, and he went through to Whitemare Pool [in South Tyneside] and he ended up at Finnigan's bar in Gateshead. That was where Viv had the fight with Paul Ashton. The fight went on up the road for about 20 minutes. They reckon Billy Robinson stepped back to see what our Viv could perform like. Well, Viv played with Ashy for 20 minutes around the car park and Ashy was shouting and bawling at him to stand still so he could hit him. Viv was just bop-bopping; he was like greased lightning.

'Then he went to work at Wheelers, on the Gateshead side of the Tyne Bridge, just before you go over on the left-hand side; it's closed down now. [Wheelers has since been demolished to make way for new development near Gateshead Quays.]

'He was with Billy Robinson then. The problem was, Viv was from the sticks and the townies didn't like this. They would say, "Where's he from? What!" A lot of them had the idea that no one was going to come in from the sticks and do anything to them, sort of thing.'

Hazel talked of Viv's childhood, about when he had run-ins with his peers: 'I used to fight his battles. Viv wouldn't fight.'

Jack offered up a story about Viv's childhood: 'He fought out there with young Stubbsy, and Stubbsy was knocking hell out of him. I said, "I'll bloody murder you, lad, for letting him do that to you. Give him some back!"

'I used to take him to boxing and he took to it like a duck to water. He had four things going for him that very few fighters have got – I mean street-fighting. He had speed, he had the wind, the stamina and he had the hitting power. Put them on that street or a football field and phew! They just couldn't put it together, they don't know how to use their hands, and they depend on just strength and weight. You can be as strong as a bull, but, if you're not fit and once you start puffing and panting, then you're finished. You're fighting some bugger and you start puffing and panting and he's still going strong! It's time for you to reverse because you're going to get a tousing. Viv knew how to hit and the weight training gave him the strength. He put four down in less than four seconds. Four blokes in the bar.

'Anna's dad come up to Viv and said, "I was just going to give you a hand there, Viv."

'Bump, bump, bump, bump! Four left hooks and they didn't get up! Mind you, I'm not just saying that because he was my lad.'

What were Viv's fears? Hazel answers this by saying, 'You know something: he was the most scared person of the dark. He was petrified, petrified!'

Jack says, with laughter in his voice, 'He would come in through the night, and to go out the room he would open that door, put that light on, and there's a switch to the top of the landing, he would put that light on. He would fly up the stairs and get a hold of his bedroom door and hoy it wide open. Then he'd knock the switch on and go in.

'One night I said, "Oh, Viv, feed them dogs, son."

'"Aye, right you are, Father."

'He would go out the back, and I would sneak out of the front door and sneak down the garden; it was pitch black! He would shout at the dogs, "Howway!"

'I would go, "Urghhh!"

'The tins and the food would go up-a-height and he's back in here like a shot.'

We all burst into laughter at the thought of this and

luckily we are all on the same wavelength to be able to enjoy a magic moment of nostalgia.

Jack went on to speak of when he and his son went shooting and how good a shot Viv was. Game pie and salmon were things that people took for granted in rural areas, and shooting, hunting and fishing are their way of life.

Hazel looked across to Viv's sister and said, 'She seen him a few days before he died, didn't you, Karen? She said, "What's wrong with your face today?"

'He said, "Oh, I'm just fed up, Karen. I'm on my way home. I'm sick of paying bills."

'Viv had just bought a house at the time.'

We talked about the Angel of the North and an article that appeared in the *Telegraph* that depicted the people of Gateshead as being thick for having the monumental sculpture. This sort of bombastic approach to public art goes against all that northerners have fought against for many years. Hazel said of the Angel, 'It's horrible.'

Jack's view was: 'I think it's a waste of space myself. The people of Gateshead had no bloody choice in the matter. It was the council that made the decision.'

While we were on this subject, Viv's artistic ability came up and Jack said, 'I think he was a bit thicker than me when he was at school. It was only in my last three years at school that I picked up and I think Viv did the same. Viv was obsessed with strength. He started with a Bullworker [fitness training device] and when he was working he would put six more bricks in a hod than anyone else and it just went on from there. He looked far bigger stripped than he did with his shirt on.

'What I put it down to is these old cowboy films: the gunslinger. There's always somebody wants to take your reputation. Well, as he went on, his reputation just grew and grew and more blokes tried to take it off him. He wasn't like a bully.

'Viv used to hold his head and say to himself, "Why is that man trying to have a go at me?"

'Viv would say to me, "I was sitting there having a quiet drink and another one kicked off."

'I would ask him if he won and Viv would reply, "Oh, aye! I've knacked him; you can't even go for a quiet drink, there's always somebody wanting to have a go at you, man."

'He used to go out with Anna and they would say, "He's on his own, we'll get him while he's on his own."

'He just got the reputation as a fighter and you've always got somebody to tell you what they think of you.'

What about the fighting over the insurance payouts? From what Jack said, it seems that money has been the key issue for a number of people and it cut through Jack's heart so much so that he said, 'I'm only pleased the grandbairns stayed with us on a Friday and Saturday night long before all of this happened. I've done it for donkey's years; otherwise the buggers would be saying, "They're just getting the grandbairns in to see if they can get into any money."

'But they cannot say that because the bairns have been staying long before this insurance wrangle.'

Jack is not concerned over which of his many grandchildren stay, and sometimes they have had five or six there on a Friday night.

Hazel said something that could be the answer to what has kept their spirits alive: 'It is our grandchildren that have kept us going, we look after Karen's and Martin's children because they work. Our Viv's two boys come down and

Eric's oldest boy doesn't come down because he's too big. But we always have five of them, don't we?'

As she looked to Jack for confirmation, he said in his best Geordie twang, 'Wy aye. We wouldn't have it any other way. Viv and Dean used to live only a stone's throw away, but now they've moved further away they come on a weekend.'

When we talked of Viv's commitments to others and how he had to be in a number of different places at one time, Jack said, 'Viv passed his driving test first time and he was a crackerjack! He wanted to be here before he got there. If he were going along the road he would say, "I've got to get past him, he's too slow!"'

'Not doing anything daft, no, not stupid risks, but he had to be away and that bloody thing he had, like, it would catch pigeons, man. It wasn't a big old Mercedes or a fancy BMW; it was just a Sierra Cosworth. It had a 2.9 injection engine in it. It was a flying machine; there was nowt swanky about it.'

Viv's heroes? 'Just his dad, he worshipped his dad, nobody else,' said Hazel.

Jack was overcome with embarrassment and said in a low tone, 'I never heard him.'

What he meant by this is that Viv did not openly say soft, namby-pamby things. But the point was taken about who Viv looked up to.

Jack continued, 'He liked the film *Zulu*. He watched that over and over again. It's a cracking picture.'

'He loved home cooking,' said Hazel. 'He used to get me to do a spotted dick pudding, put it in the cloth and dish and he used to say to me, "Now, Mother, how long does this take to cook?"'

'And he used to take it back with him to Daisy Hill and

cook it down there. Christmas cake, I think everybody in Daisy Hill had a Christmas cake off me. Scones, pork pies: I think I kept Daisy Hill in them. The minute they came out of the oven he would pinch them.'

Viv's grandmother stayed at Jack and Hazel's home for about five years after her husband died and eventually she got a little place near her son's home. Viv had great reverence for older people.

'Viv was obsessed with his grandmother,' said Hazel.

Jack was more expansive: 'Viv would take her all over in the car, up to the dam and down the coast. My mother would sit on a clothesline and go to hell and back if it was a ride out. I used to say to her, "I'm going to Keswick tomorrow with the wagon." Her parents belonged over there in Maryport. I used to go over, take her up and get her in the wagon.'

Viv used to train at an austere place in Highfield called 'The Hut'. Jack explained: 'It's just a hut, there's no running water or nowt like that, just up the steps, a door in, benches and weights and all the local lads go in there and train. You would just come home and have a bath or a shower after a session in there. It's got a brick foundation with wood sides. When it first started off, it was the St John's Ambulance Brigade base.

'When they started the weight training, they asked if they could use the bottom end of the hut; the other end was all stretchers and that sort of thing. Then the St John's Ambulance just sort of seemed to die out; nobody went to it and the lads took it over and paid the council a rate. It's been there for 20-odd years now.'

'The Hut' is indeed still there and what an unbelievable sight, the sort of place that those seeking the eye of the tiger would train in – if they were hungry enough! It's full of menacing-looking weight-training machines and other apparatus for self-inflicted torture. The facilities are few and it is the sort of place you would expect to see SAS men queuing to get out of!

I was looking at a family that was recalling all sorts of stories about Viv. The fear that was there on my arrival had been long since gone and the barriers had been broken down.

When the Reverend Martin Jackson officiated at Viv's funeral he said, 'Things have been said that maybe shouldn't have been.'

'He was a marvellous little man,' Hazel said of the clergyman.

Jack intervened: 'Do you like vicars, do you? Do you like churches? I'm an atheist, me. I'll tell you bloody well straight, the Protestants, they are two-faced, the vicars. But the old Catholic father, when I was at St Joseph's, he used to go down every day to the Townley Arms and have two pints.'

This talk of religion prompted a change of subject to the story of the late Harry Thompson. Hazel struck a serious note: 'You know, Father Conaty brought our Viv's name up in Harry's sermon.' The tragedy that struck the Connelly family was just as bad as what the Graham family suffered with the loss of Viv. The lives of both Viv and Harry were lost to needless violent acts. Harry, the brother-in-law of Anna Connelly, Viv's fiancÈe, was killed while trying to recover items stolen from his home in a burglary. He went to the home of those he suspected and a fight ensued in which he was stabbed and later died from his injuries.

What advice could the Grahams give to anyone considering seeking to make places safer for others, as Viv had tried to do? Jack's view was: 'Leave it alone because now it's a gun in life, it's not like me and you going outside and that's the end of it. They'll stab you or shoot you, or get a team up or baseball-bat you. There's nowt like that now, you cross somebody, and there's a team out the next bloody day looking for you or they cross you and you get a team out looking for them. I think a lad now had far better mind his own business because he's not going to win no battles; there are too many druggies.

'This bloody druggie business, I mean they're out there, mind, they'll stab you in the night and when they wake up in the morning, they wouldn't know they'd done it. You haven't got to be a big bloke; you can be six stone nowt. You can put a knife in somebody or shoot somebody just the same as somebody at 17 stone can. You see, a lot of these bouncers just look at a man. I know of a man, he's married and got a baby, he says, "Jacky, it's bloody crackers, man, you don't know when you're going to get a knife in you or …"

'This is what I mean! Well, the doormen, the majority of them, have got backup in a club and when they leave a club most people don't know where they live so they're safe in that respect. At the same time, it beats working for a living.

'If somebody said they were going to do something to our Viv, he wouldn't get a team together: he would go and sort it out himself. He never went with teams all over the place. That's just the way he was, he had no fear of anybody, he never carried a weapon. He never had a gun, a baseball bat or a knife – he just had his fists. If anyone had pulled a gun out on Viv, he would have stood his ground and tried to talk.'

Jack was asked about the time Viv consulted him over an offer of work from Tenerife. 'I told him to keep away from it. I said, "Just stay clear of it."

'Viv was wanted to do their fighting. Not only that, I says, "There's bloody guns and all sorts over there. It's not worth it. You stop home."

'I mean, when you're 20-odd or 30 you never think you'll get to 60, you're afraid of nobody and you never think what's going to come off. I didn't want him to go and he never went.'

(Viv was asked to get involved in timeshare protection rackets. Andy Winder, from Darlington, ran a modelling agency but decided he wanted a piece of the cake. He went into timeshare in Tenerife and paid dearly for it: he was involved in a knife fight and died. Jack was right to advise Viv to stay away from the sort of things that some people asked him to get involved in.)

Jack recalled a security company approaching Viv. 'Higgins Security, they were from Birmingham, they wanted Viv to go and see them. I told Viv to let them come to him.

'All of those people that Viv helped and made money for, they weren't friends, they were hangers-on; he was a money box for them and a minder for them, he got the money from the doors on different jobs and that's all he was. What I mean by he got them jobs is, he looked after their jobs for them. That's the way I mean he was a money box, because, if anybody wanted a lend of money, he would lend them it. Any trouble and he would go and sort it out for them. That's all he was to them, a money box.'

Of Viv's true friends, Hazel said, 'Viv had two genuine friends, Robbie Warton and Rob Bell. They both keep in touch, they come up here every so often; they are genuine people.'

It seemed from talking to Jack that he was more worldly-wise than most people in Newcastle are. How had he acquired this wisdom? 'I was as thick as a chip at school, me, lad,' he started, then Hazel interjected, 'You did the doors, though, when you were younger, you did the local dances.'

Jack went on, 'It was just the local dances; there were no nightclubs then! Chains out of the collar and that sort of thing! It was not as bad as now: you had broken bottles, chains and flick knives, but this drug business set it all off. Then you were hoyed out of the pub at ten o'clock. And you come out of the dances drunk. Now you get some of them in a right state, drinking all day and night and they are on this bloody stuff. It's a different ball game in the town.'

Hazel may well have pinpointed something that attracted Viv to his profession when she said, 'He did it for the money; there was no money here for him. He hated going out at the finish, though. He would sometimes just stay in.'

Jack defended Viv as regards people calling him a doorman or bouncer: 'He wouldn't stand at doors, it got to the point that, if he looked after a place, then he didn't need to be on the door. Those on the door would say, "Mind, Viv Graham looks after this place, kick off somewhere else, like."

'Viv suffered migraine, which he got from his mother. She suffers terrible with it. He used to take Paracetamol like a child eats Smarties!'

Was stress a contributor to these headaches as well? 'Definitely,' thought Hazel. 'Stress brought it all on. I mean, at times it was terrible. When he got that abscess and they said he was filled with steroids, what a load of codswallop! There wasn't a bit of steroid in his body. They said that about the steroid thing around about the time of his funeral.'

Jack then took up the subject: 'I said to Viv, "Why do you need that for? I'd rather be 15 stone or 14 stone or 10 stone of muscle and bone rather than be 18 stone of bloody water.

It's like carrying two stone of bloody tatties on your back."

'One minute they're 16 stone, then they're 19 stone. There was a time he had no neck, his stomach hung over his trousers and I ribbed him something rotten. He stopped doing the running; he was just concentrating on the weight training.

'I used to say, "Bloody weight training, aren't you? You want to get on that field outside the house and get running again."

'"Aye, Father, I'm going to get some of this off."

'"Well, you want to then. You'll meet a young Viv Graham, mind," I said.'

It was mentioned that Viv always used to say that he would meet someone bigger and stronger. 'That's his dad's saying,' said Hazel.

Jack explained, 'I used to say to him that there's always somebody that's going to be bigger and stronger than him or younger than him. "Bigger, stronger, better," I used to say. "It doesn't matter if you live to be 60, you cannot beat a 20-year-old or a 30-year-old."

'There's always somebody coming up. Even if you've never been defeated, there's a time in your life when there's a young 'un who is good enough and fit enough to beat you because you're getting too old.'

'So I said, "You either beat somebody that's better than you; there's always somebody in the world that's better than you somewhere, it doesn't matter who you are. Just look at your boxing. The best in the world can get beat. If you keep on with it, then the older you get there's a young 'un coming up and he beats you." It's a fact of life.'

When the talk turned to media coverage of their son, Hazel said, 'We had letters put through the door saying, "We wrote nice things about Viv, if you'd only talk to us," and things like that. I went to the graveyard and photographers were following me there! I used to go before eight o'clock in the morning to keep out of their road. I used to do all sorts to keep away from them.'

Jack added, 'I opened the door one day and they were there, the television people. I had to go to the inquest and two of them were in the street and they took my photograph; it was too late to stop them.'

Revisiting the subject of religion, Jack said with feeling, 'If I had my way, I would sack every vicar, Catholic priest, rabbi, mothers, every religion – sack them all. There's been more bloodshed and murder, bloody religion, in this world than anything else.

'My second wish: I would fetch Guy Fawkes back and give him all the bloody gunpowder he wanted.

'My third wish would be that Britain would have a ruler with bottle that would stand up to the rest of Europe. We don't want to be told by them what we can and what we cannot eat, what we can do and what we cannot do. See what I mean. On top of that, all of those asylum seekers, as soon as the boat come in, I would turn it around and say, "Back to where you belong."

'Some of them are parasites living off us. If there were no religion, then there wouldn't be any Catholics and no Protestants and there would not be Catholics and Protestants fighting in Northern Ireland. You wouldn't have Muslims and Sikhs fighting; everybody would be one, everybody would be the same.'

At this point Hazel said to her husband, with surprise in her voice, 'Do you know something? I've never heard you talk as much in months. I'm pleased Steve has visited tonight, it's done you the world of good.'

We talked about Viv's associate Terry Scott, who was there just seconds after Viv was shot. Jack said, 'When it happened, Terry said to us, "I'm your son." I've never seen him from that day to this. He just started to move in Viv's circles in the latter part of Viv's life and wasn't a mate of Viv's for years and years and years.

'When I went into that house [Anna's home] I just had to get out. Seeing that picture on the wall of the little girl having her communion, that did it for me.'

Hazel said, 'Viv could have a fight with someone and then shake hands, even with Stuey Watson. He made friends and he was invited to his birthday party, but he wasn't a party lad. He was dead old-fashioned.'

And Jack recalled, 'On a Saturday night he would go to the Railway pub in Walker [in Newcastle's East End] and he would have a nice drink.'

When we spoke about Michael Sayers, Jack said, 'He did say he had some trouble with Michael Sayers.' Then Hazel added, 'But no word of a lie, that Michael Sayers pulled into the yard one Christmas and gave us a Christmas card and £100 when Viv was in jail.'

'Everybody's all friends,' Jack said, 'but, if you fall out, you can fall out, can't you? So you're not friends any more.'

What about Viv enjoying the odd bet or two on the horses? Jack's answer was: 'I said, "You're crackers, man, put it away and salt it away."

'I asked Viv if he'd heard the story about putting his money away for a rainy day. I said to Viv, "Have you ever heard the story about the grasshopper and the squirrel?"

'He said, "No, what's that, Father?"

'I said, "The squirrel gathers all the nuts and it hides them all over the place. The grasshopper just jumps about and enjoys itself. The winter comes, the grasshopper has got nowt to eat, but the squirrel's got all its nuts to eat. You're not going to be 30 all your life; you're going to get to 40, 50 and 60. You can't keep this game up at that age."

'He would say, "Aye, man, Father. I'm not bothered about when I get to that age. I'm living now, man!"

'When Viv used to go the boxing matches with Rob Owen, it was, "Will I back the red corner or the blue corner? I'll have £25 on the red corner."

'He didn't know what that kid was like; he hadn't a clue what they were like. He was just laughing and couldn't care-a-less about what happened tomorrow: live for today and let tomorrow worry about itself.

'Well, ye bugger, he was 34, but he had a good life. He had a good last ten or so years. Well, see, when I think back as well, I worked all my life and an insurance bloke came around and he said, "Get a pension out for when you retire?"

'I said, "Get away, I could be dead next week, lad. What good's that to me?"

'We won the pools at work in a syndicate.

'They said, "Buy a new wagon, man."

'I said, "When I park this wagon up tonight, I forget about it until tomorrow morning and, if there's owt goes wrong with it, then he's got to fix it. I want none of that; I could be dead in five years' time."

'It's come and it's just went as the years went on, it was all spent, but when I was older it's like what I said to our Viv, I mean, maybe if I had invested that money or joined a pension scheme I would have had a good pension. I said the same as Viv and he was just doing the same stroke.'

On the subject of finances, it's good to be able to report

that since this interview took place a number of settlements have been made by insurance companies in Viv's case and various claims on his estate have been settled by legal means.

17

THE MAN WHO
INVENTED BOTTLE

Peter Connelly is the man who really holds the keys to the riddle of what made Viv tick. Peter, who was Viv's business partner and would have been his brother-in-law if events had not taken such a tragic turn, started our talk by asking if Andy Webb had been interviewed. 'He was really close to him,' he said.

Viv always blamed Andy for being the father of a child that Julie had conceived while Viv was in prison and Andy had been driving Julie to visit Viv. Viv put one and one together and came up with three, as he himself was actually the father of the child!

Peter said, 'He [Andy Webb] came here and he was crying, and he asked if I would take him across to Viv's graveside and he knelt there and sat there for an hour crying, showing his feelings.'

A number of years ago, Andy Webb held the Mr Great Britain title in the heavyweight division of the body-sculpture competition and has interests in leisure facilities around Newcastle. But, no matter how hard these heavily muscled men tried to get to Viv, Peter was closer than any friend of Viv's; he was nearly a relation and that gave him a status above that of a friend.

'People would get in contact with me to ask Viv if he would come and look after their pubs,' Peter explained. The breweries would say, "Get in touch with Peter Connelly, he'll see his brother-in-law, maybe he can sort something out for you."

'We did it in a fair way. We didn't say either, "You give us this" or "Pay us X amount of pounds and I'll look after your pub."

'All the publicans drank with me in this pub and if they had a problem they would come to me. If you had five or six characters in your bar and they want to make it into a loud bar, noisy bar, and start effing and blinding and swearing, then other people aren't going to use your bar, so the trade was dropping off in some of the pubs.'

(It was common knowledge that even the police passed on Viv's name to those in need of his assistance and advice about security.)

Peter was asked what would make these people come into a bar and behave in such a manner. 'It would probably be their local bar; it would be close to where they lived,' he replied. 'Lots of the pubs in Walker and Wallsend were all getting lots of trouble. A particular publican asked if I could bring Viv down. The troublemakers were pissing in glasses, urinating at the counter. They weren't great big, hard people. When Viv first came on the scene, they didn't realise his capabilities, they didn't realise how big and powerful he was until he got up to them. I saw it on one occasion when a guy said, "Peter, I've had enough of this."

'There was a particular family in the Walker area of Newcastle who weren't hard but they were a bit crackers! They are a known family, I know them and get on with them, but Viv was working for the publican.

'I couldn't say, "Viv, don't give them warnings because I know them."

'He always gave them three warnings. You got a first warning, a second warning and then after the third warning you had to be clipped.

'This particular guy used to cause trouble in quite a nice pub in Walker called the Stack, and Viv went in and got a hold of this man and within seconds – and this man was a big lad as well – the pee was running down his legs. Running down his legs! So! Even though the manager was a little bit frightened to say anything at the time, the next time the lad came in, the manager threw the lad a packet of Pampers, and everybody started laughing at this man who was supposed to be a tough guy.

'Then we would go on to another bar called the County.

'Viv would say to the publican, "What can you afford?"

'Viv didn't demand, "I want £100!" He would ask, "What can you afford?"

'And the reply was, "Fifty pounds a week, Viv. I won't miss £50 a week. If I get rid of these two particular people, then this bar will pick up again."

'So Viv went behind the bar and started pulling pints in the bar and started serving people as if it was a family pub, his pub!

'It was, "A pint of Guinness, Viv."

'Viv was laughing away and carrying on. "A pint of lager, Viv."

'And these people stopped literally, point-blank, and never went back in the bar again.

'The atmosphere was different in the pubs, the nightclubs and the social clubs. He didn't drink.' Peter says this with some admiration for Viv and then continues, 'He only drank orange juice and occasionally a Guinness; if you ever bought him a Guinness he would get really happy and enjoy himself. You could have a good laugh with him. It was great and everybody was happy.

'I got a phone call from a Bass publican; it was a pub off Norham Road, up in North Shields. This landlady had been petrol-bombed; she had a child on the premises; she couldn't take much more, but the breweries said they would pay to foot the bill.

'So obviously then we said, "Well, it's £500, it's a one-off thing and we aren't coming up every week."

'We got the address of these people who done this and knocked on their door and they were warned there and then! There was nobody got hit or anything like that and that was the end of the trouble for that publican up until Viv was shot, and then all hell broke loose! Obviously, everybody that ever got barred from pubs turned up. There was big parties, everybody went on a rampage, all those pubs got it that night.'

The British are steeped in a history of romantic attachments to so-called likeable rogues: Robin Hood, Fagin, Ronnie Biggs. Did the British public really want to see such a romantic figure locked up and the key thrown away?

Even though Peter admits he has a past criminal record of violence for two assaults and GBH, he was granted a publican's licence. He said it had seemed highly unlikely that he would ever get a licence under such circumstances. There has been a lot of conjecture as to how it came about that the police did not prevent this progression of events.

To some it suggests he was a police informer, but he firmly set the record straight: 'I was doing quite well and at that time I didn't hold a publican's licence or anything like that. The police asked to see me and I came down. They said, "Peter, it's come to our attention that you are trying to run a pub and we are thinking about letting you have your own licence."

'It was 10 or 15 years since I was last convicted. I took the wrong route and mixed with drug dealers, but at the time they were petty. They went in heavy-handed, that lot did; they burst into bars and smashed the place up and even took coffins to bars and did horrible and nasty things. I was with that clique for a short time because at that time I didn't have any money.'

The strategic placing of coffins outside pubs was a way of gaining territory for drug pushers, places they could deal from. 'It was mostly about money in those days,' said Peter. 'It was just before the drugs came in heavy and just before Viv came across here.'

Was it the days just before the end of the Harry Perry era? 'Harry was there; it was one of Harry's operations in his time. He was the boss way back then. Harry and me had quite a close relationship then. We were sent in to do the business and obviously they got the message. One way or another.'

Harry Perry, known as 'H', was considered a forerunner to the Viv days, way back in the 1960s and 1970s. H could use his fists, and he was said by some people to have a short fuse that could blow for the slightest of reasons.

Times have changed, but nostalgia about such places and names lives on in the North-East. Peter knew some of the patrons of Billy Bottos and he remembers one in particular: 'One of the greatest men that I admired, more than anything, was a man called Jimmy Walker. I was at his funeral. His father had him fighting three fights a day for a half a crown (12 ½ pence) a time; his knuckles were out here.' Peter put one cupped hand over the other to show what he meant. 'This was a great man and a great fighter in lots of respects.'

Where did these fights take place? 'These were the bare-knuckle days under Pottery Bank, under the bridge, in different places, and the Quayside. He met Viv lots of times and Viv loved him.

'Viv would sit and listen to some of his stories. And he had the greatest stories in the world to tell. I've always wished that before he died that someone would write a book about Jimmy Walker, because his stories were far greater than you could ever say about Viv. There were some belters. I would sit for hours and listen to them.

'They cut his legs off three times, you know!' Peter pointed to his own leg and said, 'There, there and there. He had fluid in his legs until, eventually, his legs were off and it was just a body that they were carrying about. He lived through all of that, but died from pneumonia a year later.'

Was he a hero of Viv's? 'He fought a Dutch man and at the bottom of the plate [winner's trophy] was inscribed: "The man who invented bottle", which was great because he was, until Viv came along, and Viv obviously to me was the man who had all the right bottle in the world and I've seen some awesome things when Viv was fighting! We once got called to a pub in North Shields where we got paid £200.

The man used to have a pub across here called the Queen's. When Viv first came to Newcastle, that was the first pub he started to run in the East End of the city. Denny Haig was working with Viv at that time.'

(Denny Haig is from Highfield, near Rowlands Gill, where Viv originated from, and he was featured in the TV investigative series *The Cook Report*.)

Peter went on to say, 'I didn't hold any grievance against Denny until what he did to Jack and I was really annoyed. I know he's quiet old, Denny, about 40-odd or 50, but Jack [Graham], to hit Jack! And Jack's never ever harmed anybody.

'They all seemed to jump on the bandwagon after Viv was gone; they all seemed to jump on his back and everybody was in his pockets! They'd only ever got money off Viv, he supplied their wages.'

It may well have been that Denny Haig was misquoted in the TV documentary about protection rackets. This led to a confrontation between him and Viv's father and all sorts of trouble, which ended in violence that would have seen Viv turning in his grave. The televised interview that Denny gave to Roger Cook was cut to shreds and portrayed what Denny had said very differently from what he actually said in one go.

Peter's ex-brother-in-law was David Lancaster, who was involved in the assault on Stuart Watson in Hobo's. 'Viv got into the wrong clique,' Peter said, 'and once he got into the wrong clique it was hard for him to get out. They used Viv to get them into Hobo's because they were barred and Viv took them in.'

It is said that, to arouse Viv's anger, a made-up story was put to him along the lines that Stuart Watson had broken the jaws of two young men and had got away with it. Whether or not Viv was told this remains a matter of conjecture.

'You could see by his [Watson's] face he knew what was going to kick off,' Peter said, then described the ensuing three-minute attack on Watson: 'Viv slung him about a bit, but Watson never went down, he blocked well and he covered well. You didn't see any photographs of Stuart Watson after it. You didn't see how bad he was.

'They went on about how heavy he [Viv] was and how he flung him [Watson] about like a rag doll, this, that and the other. I think it was just his [Watson's] jacket was too big for him. It looked worse than what it was; it was never as awesome as that. There were four tapes, four cameras, actually on this fight. You were getting the back before the front; you were getting the wrong sequence. It came out in the wrong sequence, not the way the event actually happened. It was nothing. I seen a lot worse than that.'

'Dodgy Ray' Hewitson was a former lieutenant of the Harry Perry camp and had served time in the early 1980s. It was suggested that his connection with Viv had given rise to the drug stories about Viv. When Peter first met Viv, 'Dodgy Ray' was one of Viv's closest friends. But Viv and Ray had eventually fallen out. Peter recalls: 'People would say, "Have you spoken with Dodgy Ray?"

'Any nightclub where people went to, they said, "I'm Viv's pal," just so they would get in.

'They never ever knew him from Adam; they had never ever met the man. You hear some stupid things from people.'

Viv was well known in Teesside and he would travel down there once a week to nearby Spennymoor, where a once-a-week rave was held in the Venue. I spoke with the club's DJ, who told me that Steve Forrest had taken over the

Venue, but its days were numbered as a rave scene. Peter confirmed that Viv made a weekly trip to the Venue, because 'He had to show his face to let them know he was in charge of it' and just showing his face there would prevent any trouble.

Viv's generosity, at times, was overwhelming. Pip Wright was a friend of Viv's and Viv gave him £500 on Christmas Day, a week before Viv was gunned down. Wright was hard up for cash and Viv was generous that way. Referring to this act of generosity, Peter said, 'Some people say Viv bought his own murder weapon.'

Wright comes into the scenario as a result of the allegation that he was close to Mickey 'Little Legs' Laing. Peter tells the story: 'Viv had showed Mickey Laing up a day or two before this [when Wright was given £500 from Viv]. In the afternoon, Viv grabbed Mickey and threw him on the pool table, but they were seen drinking together later on.

'Laing was close to this Pip Wright. I've never met Pip Wright to this day. I took over a pub a few months ago just before Christmas. There was a great big brick thrown through the window and it had a note attached saying, "Put through the window, the next time it will be off your head." It was signed on the brick, "Pippy Wright".

'I had never ever met him, but I knew he had got £500, but I don't know what for or anything like that, it was just a favour from Viv.'

(The story about people saying that Viv virtually bought the weapon that killed him must be viewed as an allegation only and there is no suggestion that Pip Wright had any connection with Viv's murder.)

Of Terry Scott, who held Viv's head as he lay dying on the ground, Peter said, 'I've only seen Terry Scott once since he phoned me from the hospital and said that Viv was dead. I saw him once when I went into a nightclub in the town. It was a nice summer's night and he just sat outside the door with his arms folded and he just looked at me and I walked in. It was just that we didn't have anything to talk about.'

If Viv had had a brother who saw things just like him and they had worked hand in hand like the Krays used to, or like the Richardsons, they would have looked out for each other if something threatened one of them. But, because Viv did not have this family support system, there was no continuity to his defence. And, although the Connellys were as close as he was going to get to a family, it was not as though they were related by blood.

But what about Viv's friends? I asked Peter. He replied, 'They were just like rats leaving a sinking ship. They were super-hard when he was there, but soon as he was gone they became nothing, they were just weaklings. He was their strength. What was going to happen to them as long as he was there? It was him that was always going to be in the front line; it was always going to be him that was going to be ...' Peter talked fast at this point, half-finishing a sentence before moving on to the next: '... they knew his capabilities and knew nothing was going to happen to them and it was just a free ride for them and there was as many as there could that got on to the bandwagon.'

The Alan Rooney case is talked about. Rooney, who was 34 in 1994, that year received an eight-year prison sentence for blackmail. In June 1993, six months before Viv was murdered, Rooney had heard of a Sunderland publican putting Viv down with insults. For these insults, Rooney was prepared to collect in the name of Viv. The sum of £5,000 was demanded and, if it was not forthcoming, Rooney told the man, he would be tortured and have his home burned down as well as being murdered. The victim was told that Rooney was acting on behalf of Viv and said, 'He's the man.'

As the victim was a father of three, his name is withheld for the sake of his children. Had Viv been a real 'up and get 'em gangster', he would have gone along to the man's home himself and done the business for the disrespect he had been shown. Viv just laughed it off like the affable man he was. Those who said he took liberties with people were proved wrong by Viv's response.

Peter commented, 'That was on the other side of the water, Sunderland. I used to like Alan Rooney, he was quite a funny lad and he came out with some funny things. When Viv was murdered, though, Alan Rooney then tried to twirl it to say he was working for Viv when that happened.

'Viv was not into blackmail and obviously had said whatever you are doing has nothing to do with me, but if you make anything from my name do it, but I am not into that.'

Peter was asked how Viv found the time to relax. 'Taking the phone off the hook for one. He used to love just getting out on the road and going somewhere different from people and maybe just him and Anna. I knew that he loved his kids and would go across as often as he could to see them. He just absolutely idolised them; there was nothing greater. I was there the day he went to the hospital when Gillian Lowes gave birth to the bairn. It was a lovely day, he was happy.

'He was a great provider for her; he never ever left her short. She always thought there was something there and that he would come back. He was a great man.'

What of the stress? 'I think Viv took too much on; he was doing far too much. Later on, drugs became a big thing and they started coming in. They weren't there at first; they started moving very fast and there were quite a few drug dealers. I didn't realise there were so many drugs about and they all wanted to be in on the nightclub scene. That's where they were sold. The Es became popular and different types of Ecstasy tablets. Viv was never involved in any type of drug dealing.'

Viv was accused, after he died, of being a big drug baron. Suggestions of a £2-million turnover and racketeering were plastered in enough newspapers to cover the side of a barn door. People say there is no smoke without fire. Most will either know someone who is a drug user or know of someone who knows someone who is a drug user. Why should Viv be any different? We live in a decadent society. Even former US President Bill Clinton drew but 'did not inhale'. But, while Viv was a naive person when it came to that side of things, he certainly did not approve of drugs. He may, though, have unwittingly become involved in activities that could have been misconstrued.

A hearsay story was related to Peter in which Viv was asked by a man in Newcastle's Madison's nightclub to sort some trouble out with two doormen who had allegedly taken his Es and his money while he was in the toilets. By all accounts, the man went crying to Viv, saying that his drugs and money had been taken from him. Viv went and knocked the doormen out and gave the man his things back.

Peter said of this, 'I don't know why he did that, but I heard about it. It was a stupid thing to do, but Viv was like that and he thought he was helping out. They weren't Viv's drugs. There was another girl in who was a big drug dealer who had plenty of money. The Sayers got involved and beat her and her man up there and then in Madison's. Viv didn't intervene; he just kept out of it. He stood back and didn't get involved in it. Then I realised that there was that many people wanting to sell drugs.

'A drug dealer asked Viv for a loan of £500. The man offered to pay Viv £600 back. I don't know if he loaned him the money, but that's the way people went on. Viv had no idea of other people's motives for wanting to borrow money.'

Peter must surely have seen a number of changes in Viv from the time he first met him up until his death? To this, he said, 'He used to love going to the gym for half an hour or an hour. He would use Andy Webb's gym and they would end up having such a laugh. The laughs that went on in the gym you haven't heard the likes of it.

'I never ever touched weights, but I was watching him as they put some weights on the bar. It was awesome, the weights they were putting on for him! Off he goes, he was bench-pressing it and it was great to see him doing this and everybody would clap and cheer. Then they would put a bit more weight on and he would just press the weight that nobody could bench-press. He used to love it if he could exceed it and get a better weight; he thought it was great.

'Each time he was getting bigger, you could see him getting bigger, but then he was getting little side-effects. He was complaining about certain things, he was aching and he didn't feel well at some stage. He had an abscess on his leg.'

Viv at this time was taking steroids and they did not agree with him as, in the end, they do not agree with anyone. Viv supposedly gave them up in response to pressure from his fiancÈe and his father.

Peter went on, 'Bad-temperedness started creeping into it. Viv didn't train as hard then. He didn't have time to train because he was running all over the place. His mobile phone number changed that many times because there were that many people who had his number.

'You would say, "Have you got Viv's number?" Then you would pass that number on to others. On my book I've got about five or six numbers for him.'

What about Higgins Security, who were apparently employed to get Viv out of a pub he was running – is this true? 'They phoned Viv up and asked to meet him and he met them and took them for dinner. They actually wanted Viv to work for them, the Higgins Security Company.'

They were called in through a North-East pub, a Newcastle pub, and it was suggested to Peter that the pub did this to stop Viv going in. 'They couldn't stop Viv from entry! I knew that he had a meeting and had to go to Birmingham, but he didn't go.'

I recalled a story I was told, which was that Viv had slapped one of the Higgins crew around and they all left after giving Viv some money. The other story was that a publican called in Higgins Security because Viv was causing some trouble. They went to see Viv and told him not to go into the pub and Viv complied. Was this right? I asked Peter. 'Viv wouldn't go down [to Birmingham], they offered to take him for a meal and meet him and obviously give him a bite of the cherry; they knew he was the only one up here who could control the doors.'

Peter recounted how Higgins Security men were controlling the doors of certain places in Newcastle. The men working for such a lucrative company had to abide by the company's wishes, but they were frightened while in the Tyneside area.

'The guys were frightened on those doors,' Peter said, 'even though Higgins was the company. They were frightened they had to do it. Everybody was going to stick by them if there was a fight, but they didn't. Whoever got hit, got hit. In Viv's case, they tried to befriend him because they didn't want to get on Viv's bad side.'

Higgins Security is not a fly-by-night company but a very respected security firm and at times works hand in hand with the authorities.

Peter continued, 'It was costing them a lot of money to bring these people up from Birmingham and keeping them in hotels. It was costing them a lot more money than what Viv was getting.'

What were they brought in for? 'I think it was the fact that there was that many getting in for nothing in some of the clubs. They started off in some of the clubs as well as some of the nightclubs; they seemed to get bigger and bigger.'

Here we have a reputable company supplying their staff to work the club doors. What was the difference between this company and Viv? Just because a company is registered does not mean it is any better or more above board than an individual employed privately for the same service. Viv was consequently asked to help Higgins out.

Peter said, 'You could see that they wanted nothing to do with Viv when he went to the places. You could see that the fear of the thought of him coming to the places put the fear of God into them. There was never any trouble. Viv didn't cause trouble for the sake of causing trouble.'

What about those people who started Viv off in the game, Paddy Leonard and Billy Robinson? 'They all get old, they've lived their lives, they just want an easy life, they just want to retire, you see. That's it, basically, and live their lives in Tenerife.'

Viv did some good in his life and supported many sports,

sponsored football teams and had a heating system installed into Wallsend Boxing Club, is this right? 'It was for a lad called Alan Malarkey who ran the club; they were a good club who were tremendous in the way of amateurs. Viv used to like to go training with the young 'uns. When they seen him it used to really cheer them up, they thought it was great.

'Another thing that was said, what Manny Burgo was supposed to do to Viv in the ring. Manny was around in the amateur boxing scene the same time as Viv. I seen Manny cower away from him; he nearly died when he was caught in Macey's in the town. When Viv caught him, he couldn't get out, he shouted, "Viv! I've come to sort it out."

'Manny was more or less in charge of the coast. He didn't ever venture on to Viv's territory, but then obviously Viv got well known. It didn't stop here; it was getting bigger and bigger, so eventually these people were getting sick of the people they had paid for a long time and they wanted Viv. They wanted Viv; it was as simple as that.

'People would say, "Who's he?"

'And just about everyone knew him. "They call him Viv," would be the reply.

'Then he started going into Whitley Bay, Tynemouth, and he started getting bigger pubs and clubs. They felt he shouldn't be doing this because he was cutting them out of a job.

'Viv would say, "I'll keep two of your pubs and you can have the rest yourselves."

'Manny Burgo had come into Newcastle to see Viv to sort the situation out. In Macey's there was him [Manny] and a few of his pals and he had come to try and see Viv. There was something or another said. You've never seen anybody run like Viv did! Viv was running this way and the other to try and catch him! Manny talked his way out of it and Viv gave him the benefit of the doubt and didn't hit him or anything, and this man Burgo is huge.

'Manny actually got in the car to drop me off. It was never mentioned again. When Manny ever sees me now he never speaks or anything, he just walks straight past, and, mind, I watched him box, but I never rated him. He didn't ever fear me in any way and I wasn't feared of him. I'm not feared of anyone that I've mentioned, I don't fear for Adam.

'It just cut everybody up; he didn't deserve it.'

Peter's voice went dry and husky and just a hint that his inner strength was fading showed through the happy-go-lucky exterior. His point about not valuing life any more was amplified by a number of people connected to Viv. Viv seems to have been the beacon of light that led them into another world.

What about these people who made Viv Graham into what he was. Built him up and put him on a pedestal and went away and left him there. He had to be Viv Graham on his own; he couldn't be Viv Graham with Billy Robinson or Paddy Leonard?

Peter finishes off by saying, 'I think you start to meet new people and new friends. I don't think Viv ever thought to any extreme that things were going to come to him being wanted as badly by different pubs and clubs and even shops. What about the coloured community? He had to go and sort out trouble at the mosque. Viv was asked to help them resolve a situation, which he did.

'It could be argued that Viv had no colour bar when it came to money but the fact is Viv had no discrimination against any race or colour. What if Viv had been a member of the National Front? Would that have made the press happy enough? There were no reports of his do-good actions by the press because it just didn't sell newspapers.'

CONTACT FROM BEYOND
THE GRAVE

When I called on the services of a clairvoyant/medium, little did I know what I would be getting into. What follows is an account of what occurred in 1997. It was a direct result of my determination to seek the assistance of a spiritualist medium in order to make contact with Viv. Make of it what you will; I do not ask you to believe or to disbelieve anything in this chapter. But I was a witness to what happened and I am happy to state that what I heard on a remarkable audiotape is accurately reproduced here.

During the course of my hypnotheric travels (I don't want to bore you with the details, so I'll get this part over with as fast as I can) I would book space at Mind, Body and Spirit events to promote my particular type of Groverian therapy, adopted from a man called David Grove. No doubt he will be surprised to get a mention in a 'gangster' book I wanted to see how mediums worked, I was not sceptical of

Groverian therapy, but very sceptical of the methods of mediums... I used my therapy stall to get nearby to them to see what it was all about, and I found out their patter was water. Many cranks and fakes are about, ready and willing to take your money. There would be about half a dozen so-called mediums in attendance, sitting waiting for the gullible or hopeful punter who quite willingly parted with £10 for a five- or ten-minute reading and a further tenner to prolong the agony. I would hear the same mediums, hour after hour, use the same ploy on the willing punters. 'There's something connected with your hands, dear. Let me see, have you had some joint trouble?'

'No.'

'Well, has there been someone in your family who has had hand trouble? Maybe they were left-handed or something like that?'

'No.'

'Well, has there been someone you know who has had hand trouble?'

And so it went like that all day, yawn, yawn. By the end of the day's session, I felt ready to take any fare-paying punter on board for a five-minute tour of their Great Auntie May's rendition of 'Knees Up, Mother Brown' – for a tenner, of course.

I must point out that there are some very genuine mediums about, but in all honesty they are as rare as rocking-horse shit.

Spiritualists are reviled and hated by the Church because they are seen as incompatible with religious belief and as having direct contact with the devil. This is the view of not just one Church but a whole array of faiths. The Bible forbids the practice of spiritualism. Why? Because there must be some truth in spiritualists having gifts and powers to contact the other side. Why is the church so keen to advise against this type of activity? It is said that God forbids his people to consult mediums and if this is true there must be some truth in what mediums reveal.

One of Jesus's disciples met a medium and cast out the evil spirit that supposedly controlled her. The New Testament condemns the practice of spiritualism. The message is that there is a prohibition on the dead communicating with the living. Yet Jesus rose from the dead and appeared to his disciples, which would seem to be contact with the living made by a man that was dead. I do not intend to get involved in religious arguments here, but simply to set down some of what has been said against this kind of activity.

It is true that spiritualism, like other occult practices, can be used for good or for bad purposes. In my investigation, the good side was called on. The spirits of the dead are supposedly called up and contact is made with them. You can decide for yourself about the truth of this claim after reading this chapter. I, for one, kept an open mind about the benefits of the medium's craft in this serious investigation.

To bring this back to the context of crime, as it is the murder of a man we are concerned with, some police forces in the UK have used the services of spiritualists and the USA is awash with co-operation of this kind. The gifted lady I found is here given the name 'Crystal'; this is not her own name, as she asked that it be changed. Crystal asked for no fee or free publicity. She did not know who Viv Graham was and had no prior knowledge of his activities throughout the North-East. I concluded that she was not in it for the money or free publicity, but she did say, when asked, that if anyone wished to contact her they could do so through the publisher, who would pass on their details.

The first port of call in our investigation was the murder site of Viv Graham; next was Anna Connelly's home; and finally the spot where the killers dumped their blue Ford Escort getaway car. In order to help Crystal make a connection, articles belonging to Viv were given to her, which she held close to her while she sat in the rear of our makeshift mobile office – a car.

It was a quiet, dull Sunday afternoon. In order for you to understand that what will be revealed later on was not orchestrated, let me tell you about the set-up. The event was audiotaped from start to finish with my trusty portable recorder and specially adapted microphone lead. This recorder, which had never let me down before, had decided to develop some faults when the tape was relayed to a master tape. The results were eerie, to say the least. Batteries were replaced with new ones before every interview. They could last up to eight hours if need be, but were replaced after each interview, or every four hours if the interview took longer. These precautions ensured that no interview material was lost. Transfer of the original tape to the master tape was done in real time, to ensure that there was no loss of sound quality.

A female researcher brought something to my attention and asked me to listen to a part of the recording that had shocked her. I am not one to be easily shocked or moved by things that at first appear strange. My previous involvement in a number of eerie happenings and hearing underworld confessions had case-hardened me. But nothing could have prepared me for what I was about to hear! I once believed that everything could be explained, but as I listened to that particular section of the tape over 100 times I reached the conclusion that what I had heard was not manufactured and could not have been.

I was present at all times when Crystal was with us. I had full control of the audio recorder and the tape never left my possession until I placed it in the dubbing machine ready for one of my researchers to transfer the recording. Up until now I have never publicly revealed what sent shivers up my spine when listening to this particular part of the tape. Before we consider it, I must stress that I do not want to create a sensation. I have no need to do that as I have achieved all that I can during my writing and publishing career. I have nothing to gain. On the contrary, I risk being mocked for what I am about to reveal. Nor do I wish to hurt the memory of Viv or his family. We are talking about a man whose family love and miss him immensely.

A conversation and Crystal's narrative on what she is sensing is clearly heard. Then a sort of background interference comes in: wailing, roaring, in slow motion. A deep-throated roar of pain is clearly heard and it goes on for several minutes! There is no other way to describe it, and it is not a trick. Every single time I listened to this roaring and wailing, involuntary shivers travelled up and down my spine. I wasn't in fear, but I sensed something was trying to communicate with us. None of this sound was around us when we recorded the session, but something very strange had happened and Crystal hurriedly asked me to drive away.

We are sitting in Border Road, Wallsend, just feet from where Viv was gunned down; near to Head Hunters barber shop!

Crystal says, 'He wasn't the least bit surprised by who murdered him. He didn't give it a second thought about who the people were, as he actually expected the people to behave like that, so, instead of telling anybody, he assumed that people would have known. He was definitely thick-headed the night he died from some cause.'

What Crystal says here fits in with what Anna Connelly had told me, some weeks before, of her suspicions that Viv had been spiked to slow him down.

Crystal continues, 'In some form, it was affecting his concentration and annoying him, irritating him. Could he have had any premonition that this was going to happen?'

She is told that Viv said he would die before he was 40 and that he just lived for the day.

Crystal is right in what she says about Viv knowing who his killers were. For when he talked with his prospective brother-in-law, Peter Connelly, about who he thought was most likely to kill him, Viv actually named the people who were responsible and Peter named someone who was responsible in some way for putting the plot together. Crystal is correct about that and confirms what had been found out.

She asks, 'Had he had a previous head/neck injury at the back of his head?'

Viv's frozen shoulder was the only known injury near his head and neck, although he did suffer from pounding headaches.

'That would affect his neck. I get a very great impact from his boxing on his thought processes. He could be very quick-witted and also could be very thick, a very funny combination,' says Crystal with an outburst of breath between her words.

This shows me she is focused on the task.

Crystal: 'I think the glass was already gone in the car and

that was supposed to be something to disguise something.'

This ties in with the warning that Viv was given about the consequences of coming back to his car to find a popped window or a flat tyre and dilly-dallying too long.

Crystal: 'That was absolutely deliberate and it was something to do with how to fire the gun, as well as something to do with not worrying about windows going up and down or something. It was a mechanical aspect of firing the gun, so it was necessary. It doesn't completely make sense to me.'

I put to Crystal, 'So if someone was to shoot from that back lane, if he had got into the car they would have had to shoot at the window and the bullet may have deflected, so do you think it may have been the concern of the killers?'

Crystal: 'The window was already out, it was quite deliberate and I would say it was almost out in a particular position as well. Going back to Viv, I'm very intrigued by how he thought because it's like he … well, he certainly wasn't your average guy in terms of his thought processes at all.'

I put it to Crystal that Viv was made into what he became and wanted to get out of it but couldn't, and those people who made him into what he became left him to get on with it and left him all on his own.

Crystal: 'He was carrying an enormous amount of tension around as well. And I would say he could be very soft and sentimental and also very aggressive as well; really a very peculiar mixture. People around him wouldn't necessarily know when and which was to come out. He would be more scared than he would be willing to admit to anybody. Also, he was pretty careful; he really did tiptoe in some groups. It didn't appear to those outside the group that he was tiptoeing around, but he did pussyfoot around people. He would come up as not very nasty and abrasive, but was also very careful.'

'So he did it in a nice way?'

Crystal: 'No! I wouldn't say so! He could be charming, but he could also be ruthless. He knew how to play things. He knew which way things would swing and, yet in some ways, he wasn't that intelligent; on mundane things he wasn't that intelligent. A very, very peculiar mixture. Is this sounding right?'

I do not verify or confirm what Crystal says, but simply say, 'That sounds like a general description of that man.'

Crystal: 'I think his body was quite a struggle to him. I think he needed to keep it very functional and yet it used to bother him a lot, particularly his shoulder and neck. He was very aware of his body being powerful and yet he didn't feel very comfortable with it either. He wanted it to be supreme, he wanted to really be powerful, to be well built, to be on form, to be like an athlete's body, and yet a lot of the time to him, even though it looked good, it didn't feel good at times. He was very aware … he almost felt disabled with it at times. The image of himself was, he wanted to be bigger but he wasn't comfortable with what he had.'

What Crystal says of Viv being trapped in the typical body-builder's syndrome, and never becoming as big as the mental picture he had in his head, rings true.

Crystal is shown some photographs of Viv after she says this, and this confirms to her that what she has said is correct. It would have been far too easy to show Crystal some photographs before we started, but that would have made this contact doubtful in terms of her description of him.

Crystal: 'He needed that image, but it didn't feel

comfortable for him. He actually felt more comfortable with his body when it wasn't like that. I think that affected his thinking as well – perhaps that was the steroids?

'He got sloppy in terms of how he looked after his life towards the end. I would say his thinking processes deteriorated and he took more risks and, in a way, he was "asking for it".'

Were these risks new risks? Crystal is asked.

Crystal: 'He couldn't keep being "on guard" – it was so exhausting. Which meant that he let his guard down more in the last couple of years of his life. His thinking processes were quite seriously affected by the time he died. He wasn't as rational, he wasn't as sensible, he wasn't as clear-headed; he wasn't even thinking things through, so he was more of a target.'

She is asked about the people who did the harm and whether he knew where it came from.

Crystal: 'Yes he knew. Was one of them quite thin with quite a small jaw? I've got a vision; the top half of the person's face was bigger than the bottom with probably larger ears than should be, proportionately larger ears. Someone who didn't make total sense in terms of what he had achieved in life – a weasel-like person. Someone who was very, very confident and very, very quick-witted and very ruthless and very talented.'

Crystal is asked if the person she is describing could retort with a fast answer, or a witticism, that would fit with what she has said.

Crystal: 'Yes, yes, yes, that would fit. This person didn't control anything with his body, he controlled with his mind and his cynicism. I would say he was between 30 and 40, and very thin in his youth. He was very, very capable of ruling people. He certainly had no concerns for other people. That puzzles me clairvoyantly how, with those looks, he could command the position that he got to. A powerful man with a lot of luck on his side to get to that position, with a lot of shrewdness. Someone who completely understands how to play people off against one another, without getting caught.'

Crystal can actually read my mind; 'thought processes' would be a better description. This helps very well as it cuts down the need to explain things in detail to her. Without any prompting, she says, 'It doesn't fit what you're thinking.'

What has confused me here is that I am wondering who Crystal is describing, because I have something else on my mind. Usually this doesn't show and I can think bilaterally while listening. Crystal knows my thoughts do not match what she has been saying and lets me know. This was my first indication that there was more to Crystal than met the eye and I was beginning to wonder if what she was saying could be right.

I go on to say, 'Now wait a minute! You've got something right there: it fits the party who I believe gave the money and other payment for the killing ...'

Crystal interjects and says emphatically, 'Yes, yes, yes.'

I continue, 'That's who it fits, that's right, that's right, it does fit. I thought you meant the actual person responsible, the perpetrator of the crime. You are right, because the face and the features you describe ...'

Crystal again interjects, saying, 'I'm describing the person that ordered it. Even before I arrived here, I've got the person and if you showed me a photograph of them I could say "yes" or "no". If someone gave me an Identikit, I could do it. He wasn't always well shaven and he had his hair pretty short at the time and it was brownie, mousy-coloured. He had a very black and white outlook and wouldn't wear colourful clothing and, I don't know why, but you wouldn't catch him out wearing bright types of clothing.

'Two people were told to do the hit. If they hadn't succeeded they would have been very thoroughly tripped up and left flat on their faces. I think something would happen to their feet or their ankles. I don't know why, it's not knees, it's lower; ankles. They would have had their faces damaged if they didn't succeed; they would have had their faces smashed in first. These people were terrified, absolutely petrified, and very similar in terms of how they dealt with it. They thought in a very similar way, were they brothers?'

My reply is that they were very close. It is explained that the people responsible and a few others had got wind that people had wanted Viv out of the way.

Now this is the part that fits in with the wailing and pained roaring on the audiotape.

Without warning, Crystal says, 'I think we need to move away from here.'

I said, 'Do you think?'

Crystal: 'Yeah! We can't continue here, sorry, I just feel like we do ...'

I get my seat belt on faster than normal and speed off in the 7 Series BMW, feeling uncertain about what Crystal meant. I believe she has felt something or spotted something in one of her mind pictures and I'm not hanging around to find out what it is, because at this stage the atmosphere is becoming a bit charged and the area around Crystal has become very steamed up, yet my windows are clear. It looks as though she is surrounded by a mist, although that is not the case.

We then head towards Anna Connelly's home and park nearby.

Crystal: 'You were talking, weren't you?'

'I was, actually, then you just said ... do you think somebody phoned the police and ...?'

Crystal interjects, 'I don't know, I just ... somebody phoned somebody. I'm not sure if it was the police. I just didn't want to be ...'

She fails to finish what she started to say and I feel it is something more sinister, but I do not wish to add things that were not said.

Crystal: 'Anyway, I needed to comment on something you were saying. Oh, yes. It was about, were they brothers? They certainly think in the same way.'

I ask if they were frightened of failure.

Crystal: 'Horrified! They had been given some specific instructions, but the rest they had to work out for themselves; they were petrified. I would say the specific instructions were in terms of weapon, window down, what they yelled at Viv.'

Was there something particular they had to yell to Viv?

Crystal: 'Yep, something very derisory. They were also told locations not to risk and areas that were safe. This was a second or third time they wondered about doing it. They had one firm try and one other one that they aborted and then this was the third attempt.'

Did Viv have any awareness of this and what made them abort the second attempt?

Crystal: 'They aborted after a police presence. Not a police presence that was actually relevant, but they aborted.'

The police higher up the chain of events, but was there a reason why they didn't do this themselves?

Crystal: 'Yeah! They would have been linked too strongly; they would have been too obvious, so this one had to be delegated, even if it had to be delegated to a buffoon. In a way, they were actually expecting these two to get caught, but the person that ordered it would have been quite happy for them to be caught. He actually thought they were such idiots that they would actually get caught and these two thought they would get caught too. Somehow they managed not to. I think they were very lucky not to. They were terrified because they were caught between the devil and the deep blue sea.

'The people involved in the killing had a meeting with those that wanted it done and, when they were approached, they would have looked foolish if they had backed out. They weren't approached, but told. They were allocated the job. Like in a social strata or hierarchy, they were in a lower level. The hitmen responded to orders. They weren't on an equal footing with the man I described as a weasel.'

Crystal is uncannily close to the description of one of the main persons suspected of being responsible. Her description of 'a weasel' will probably stick and time will tell if this is the correct person. (Later a photograph was forwarded to Crystal of this man and she confirmed that it was indeed the picture she had in her head of the man who gave the instructions to the two killers.)

She says she is trying to get a picture of those in the car. 'One of them had quite curly hair, dark brown. These two have a sense of humour. They could mix sociably better; the weasel had a sarcastic sense of humour, but no real proper sense of humour, a very nasty sense of humour, a very bitter sense of humour as well.

'On the personality side, the weasel guy is far more

psychopathic and the other two were very much in denial, like, "I don't think I did it, so I didn't do it," sort of thing. Believing that, if they didn't think about it, then they hadn't actually done it – they were kidding themselves.

'There is some dodgy stuff in the police around here!'

I ask, 'In terms of what?'

Crystal: 'Being paid?'

It is pointed out that there are links between police and big-time criminals, which is proven by anti-corruption ploys within certain police forces.

Crystal mentions a police officer, although not by name: 'Quite high up, but not at the top. He's quite a solitary person.. There are lots more people involved in this than the ones we are talking about. The death changed the power balance and when things happen, they act accordingly. The police know the scenario, but haven't pursued it heavily because they also have to pursue other things. The police trade both ways, they trade, they catch them out, trip them up, lock them away. There's three ways they play; they play that way and put different levels of pressure on to keep certain levels of violence and certain levels of crime under control.

'Dodgier all the way, as well. Different levels of strata here, they are certainly not clean.'

Did Viv know his killers?

Crystal: 'I would say he knew both of them; he would have recognised them more as messengers rather than as paid to do it, rather than ordered to do it, rather than they deciding to do it themselves. He had dealings on and off with them, but he knew of a lot of people.'

Crystal is asked whether, if she were given the initials of the killers, she would be able to communicate and confirm the initials were correct.

Crystal: 'I think it would be better if I try to describe them. We'll start with the one with curly hair. One has got curly hair that has at sometimes been curlier than at other times. Brown to black with hands that are quite grazed and rubbed on the knuckles and rings on the middle fingers, but not on the outside fingers.

'Aged late twenties to early thirties when it happened. Someone who could be very rough with a girlfriend, he threatened to strangle her. Not carrying a lot of flesh and wearing quite scruffy clothing. If there was a woman involved, she could have had blonde hair but dyed brown.'

When Viv crawled along that street after being shot, did he notice anything?

Crystal: 'Only his pain and the weight of his body, which gave him some difficulty in moving his arms because of the weight of his body. He was far more concerned with the state of his body than who had done it.'

What Crystal says is true. Viv had come to rely on his body over the years and this shooting had taken any dignity away from him in that he had to drag himself by his arms along a main road in full view of the passing public. Not just an end whereby he died instantly, but a drawn-out event where his dignity was unseated and he was left to crawl with his last remaining energy ebbing away. He knew he was about to die, but his concern was for those around him so that they would not have the indignity of seeing him die in such a state. Right up to the end, his concern was for those lesser mortals around him. Viv was concerned that no one should see him in the gutter with this wound and he tried gallantly to pull his shirt over it, as well as asking to be helped up so that he didn't look as bad.

Crystal: 'I think he felt very cold as well with the shock.'

What was Viv thinking when this happened?

Crystal: 'His only thought was to get away. He didn't care who'd done it. He hurt; it was physical ...' Crystal makes a sound that indicates a deep-seated pain.

Did Viv get the peace he craved while he was alive?

Crystal: 'I'll try and get him now. Yeah, in a way it's a relief. Also I think he was aware he was hurting people a lot and there was a part of him that just wanted out of that. So in a way, it was like, "I'm not doing anything to hurt anyone."

'Yeah! I've got him on the other side now! He's more concerned at what he's done than what others have done. Viv would be tickled pink at what you are doing. He has a nice gentle sense of humour as well, you know.

'He's such a chameleon. I would say in spirit he's more concerned about his kids not going wrong when they grow up. But he really wanted better things for them.'

It is pointed out that Viv had a number of children and that he visited them all the time. He gave them lots of things he didn't have. We have a set of his trainers with us and I point at them, explaining that Viv was happy with ordinary Dunlop trainers, cheap compared with those we have with us, but in the end it was only the best of everything: £90 trainers, £90 shirts. It was literally the best of everything, which only started when he came to live in Newcastle.

Was Viv concerned about what people thought of him in terms of money?

Crystal: 'I think he was more concerned about his body than anything else.'

We then move on and visit Anna Connelly's home and Anna explains to Crystal about how the other mediums had taken her for a ride. At first, it had helped, but then 'a lot of them were telling lies by what they had seen in the papers and they just started to make it up'.

The talk is small and there is not much time, as Anna is hurrying to go out, so we cannot make an appraisal here. Anna asks how we know we have things right, and it is briefly explained to her that because of Crystal's help we know the whole story because parts of the jigsaw are being pieced together with Crystal's help.

Whatever is hurrying Anna must be important, but she asks if Crystal can sense Viv in her home, to which Crystal replies, 'I've had quite a strong sense of him and he worries about his kids and he worries about you and the people around you. He struggled with his life and his body and in a way it's a release not to be doing that any more. There's a tremendous amount of grief at being separated from you and an incredible amount of tears and unhappiness, almost like he'd lost part of his soul. He was particularly fond of your daughters as well. His spirit feels very resolved compared to some people I see. I think he was always aware that he was going to go and that helped him prepare to some degree. So when it happened it wasn't like, "Oh, my God. This wasn't supposed to happen." So in that way I think it helped him resolve things more easily.'

Anna says, 'You're right there, he knew it was going to happen and he wanted to go, and it was a relief to him; he had constant headaches all the time.'

Crystal: 'Does it come from the back of his neck, the headaches?'

Anna: 'Yes, he always had tension across on his shoulder. He had a bad shoulder as well.'

Crystal: 'I know he tried to carry more weight [extra body weight]. Did it feel uncomfortable as well?'

Anna gives a contradictory reply, and later on it is shown to be so: 'No, he liked carrying weight, the more the better.'

Crystal: 'I think it was good for him that he looked like that. I think he didn't actually like the feel of that much, maybe he hadn't told you.'

Anna: 'He didn't, because he liked running and he couldn't run with that weight on him, so yeah, maybe it could be right, maybe he never told me that bit. What else? Is he happy?'

Crystal: 'I certainly get a much happier feeling than the two years before he passed over, because he struggled with himself in the last two years a lot. I get a strong sense of resolution around it. I've had people that come through to me and have told relatives to eff off because they're not resolved; he's not in that category. He's looked at himself and he's worked through it, but he's still very concerned about the people he loved. Very, very concerned, and you haven't coped very well and he's struggled with that.'

Anna: 'I have now, these last nine months I have, but not before, I didn't. I think he's moving on anyway because that's the feeling I get. He's happier now.'

Crystal: 'There are different stages up there. He worries about you.'

Anna: 'I'm just glad he's happier, in a happier place than where I am, I'm telling you.'

Crystal: 'I've had a good link with Viv today.'

On playback, what is a very good-quality tape, recorded on my Panasonic recorder, shows signs of slowing down and then increasing in speed. There is also a lot of electrical interference and static on the tape, which has not happened before. The tape speed returns to normal for no apparent reason. Make of that what you will. Again, the master tape is kept for reference purposes.

We are now off to visit the site where the killers dumped their getaway car. The place in Simonside Terrace, Heaton, now has houses built on what was once a strip of wasteland. So we are parked as close to it as we can get.

When the tape is replayed it is found that it has recorded at about three-quarters speed. Once again, there is no clear reason. No doubt, some university professor will come along and give a million explanations, such as flat batteries, power surges, poor-quality tapes, electric current in the atmosphere, and so on.

This could be looked upon as some scientific experiment but I do not go in for that sort of thing as it is above me. What I do go in for, though, is something called the sixth sense; for example, when you know who it is that is calling when your telephone rings and you pick up the receiver and say their name.

The tape is so full of static interference and poor sound quality that I can only interpret snippets, as will be clear from what follows.

No one spotted the killers leaving the car or going to another vehicle. It was reported, though, that a female was nearly knocked over by the getaway car as it sped around the corner towards where we are now.

Crystal: 'I haven't really described the other guy.'

Crystal describes something intimate about this man that is withheld on her advice. Although it is now over eight years since Crystal gave that instruction to me, I still adhere to it.

I ask, 'Is there a woman, erm …?'

Crystal finishes what I was about to say, '… in common … no. But I think you might think there is.'

This woman is just incredible! She has taken the thought right out of my head and that has set my sixth sense off. I have not had this happen to me before, and I say, 'I do think they did actually, yeah! That's right. It's uncanny. I'm starting to get tingles.'

Crystal is laughing and she is on full power at this site. I start to think to myself that there are certain things I have not to think about in this woman's presence. This is not some stage show. It is for real; we are really doing something and I cannot help but feel what Crystal is saying comes directly from a connection she has made with Viv.

My guess was that Viv had warned off one of this lot from his territory of Wallsend, Shieldfield and Byker over a woman. I embroider this with the full details so that Crystal has a background to my thoughts.

She slams my theory when she says, 'It's not true; they didn't have a woman in common. One of the men still has a score to settle.'

We now have a pinging sound, like an echo-finder on a submarine, interfering with the sound quality. An electrical whirring sound is heard, but that is clearly coming from the electric window being lowered. Now we sound like the Smurfs talking. Interpreting what has been said is now difficult, but, to give you the gist of it, Crystal intimates that the killers left the car quickly but within a short time decided to set fire to it, although this was not a part of the original plan. Now the sound quality is returning to normal and the Smurfs have left us.

Crystal: 'I query when the car was set alight. I think the killers came back later to do it.'

I ask about the gun.

Crystal: 'The gun is a bit of a talking point and is still around.'

Crystal says something that is very important for her, but over the top of that I hear a sound on the tape recording that I know is wailing.

Crystal says: 'I'm clear that one of the killers is presently free, so I don't particularly want to describe him in any further detail for my own safety.'

There is a third person, Crystal says, and, quite audibly on the playback of the recording, a howling sound is heard but much more clearly than the previous wailing. I can sense a whole pack of animals listening in the background, which is spasmodically littered with the howling and wailing sounds.

The same recorder and same tape were used after this and there were no 'special effects' on the tape: it was quite clear.

Crystal has not asked for any fee, she does not advertise and does not need the work from any publicity as she has enough to keep her going.

CONCLUSION

When you have done an experiment there has to be a conclusion. In this case, there is no conclusion. I sat for many months, on and off, through the Freddie Knights murder trial at Leeds Crown Court. I have interviewed nearly 400 people about Viv's murder. I have discovered things that I never intended to. But I have no conclusion.

You will recall Lee Watson goading the police about how they could not catch Viv's killers; we have heard claim and counterclaim as to the identities of Viv's killers; but still no conclusion.

The feuding over insurance payouts has been concluded. The feuding over the house Anna and Viv lived in has been concluded. The denial and counter-denial as to the paternity of Viv's children has been concluded. The feuding among the three women in Viv's life has been concluded. But not his death.

Catching the killers would be an exercise in good policing, but most in the know already know the identity of his killers and it may only be a matter of time before they dish out their own instant justice, as the chances of the police bringing any charges are now very slim indeed.

I know nothing but feelings of sadness about those who promised to give their permission to allow their characters to be used in a big-screen movie and then withdrew that promised permission when I had £3 million of funding in place. There would have been a big payday for Viv's children.

ACKNOWLEDGEMENTS

Many thanks to the following family members of Viv for their support: Jack and Hazel Graham, Anna Connelly, Peter Connelly, Sharon Tate, Karen (Viv's sister) and various other family members too numerous to mention.

A particular thanks to the girlfriend of the late Lee Duffy, Lisa Stockell, and his many friends, who wish to be nameless.

Particular thanks also to certain officers of Northumbria Police Force for their unselfish efforts to have the killers of Viv Graham brought to justice.

I would like to thank those involved in the production company Dryden Harley Productions Ltd for their efforts in creating a film script and seeking funding for a cinema movie.

A final thanks to the many hundreds of people who gave their time to be interviewed and for the information anonymously sent by those not wishing to be named.

VIV GRAHAM

Information on the murder of Viv Graham or any other murder can be given to Crimestoppers by calling 0800 555 111 (Freephone, UK only).

01142442313

www. على استمتعبلد og.com